Being Church,
Becoming Community

Being Church, Becoming Community

JOHN M. BUCHANAN

Westminster John Knox Press
Louisville, Kentucky

Book design by Jennifer K. Cox
Cover design by Alec Bartsch

First edition

Published by Westminster John Knox Press
Louisville, Kentucky

This book is printed on acid-free paper that meets the American National Standards Institute Z39.48 standard. ⊛

PRINTED IN THE UNITED STATES OF AMERICA

97 98 99 00 01 02 03 04 05 — 10 9 8 7 6 5 4 3 2

Library of Congress Cataloging-in-Publication Data Is Available

ISBN 0-664-25669-4

96-20252

To Sue

Contents

Preface

We stood in line, four of my five children and I, looking west, over the expanse of Chicago, stretching all the way to the horizon. We were standing in the observation area of the John Hancock Building, ninety-five stories above Michigan Avenue. The occasion was a farewell to the city we all loved and that, in different ways to be sure, had formed each of us. Sue and I had come to Chicago as newlyweds, to begin our life together in Hyde Park as I entered the Divinity School of the University of Chicago and Chicago Theological Seminary. The four children with me had been born at the University's Lying-In Hospital. My first pastorate was in Dyer, in the Calumet region of Northern Indiana. Then we lived in Lafayette, Indiana, for eight wonderful years, all the while within easy reach of Chicago's vigorous culture. We read the city's news-papers, watched its television stations, made regular trips to the city for Grant Park concerts, theater, and shopping.

Now we were moving away, to Columbus, Ohio. So we planned a festive if nostalgic trip to say good-bye. The day had begun at Lincoln Park Zoo and would come to its glorious conclusion in Wrigley Field to see the Cubs play the Pittsburgh Pirates. In between we planned to visit the Hancock Building, completed not long before and the object of my children's admiration and fascina-tion from afar. And so, there we were, the five of us—Sue and our youngest in his stroller were waiting at ground level—looking out over the city toward O'Hare, fascinated by the size and strength, a little in awe actually. Our eyes followed the city from the horizon to the very foot of the building on Michigan Avenue, which can be seen if you are courageous enough to lean into the glass of the observation tower and look straight down. There in the concrete and steel canyon, at the base of a one-thousand-foot vertical drop, was a church. From the Hancock tower it looked like a miniature, its gothic architecture gracefully fragile, its green courtyard with a tiny, shining fountain in the center, a small jewel.

"Daddy, there's a church down there," my son said.

"Yes," I responded, "there's a church down there, a big famous church, Fourth Presbyterian. A lot of wealthy people belong to that church and their ushers wear fancy coats and striped pants," I explained, repeating the Fourth Church lore (stereotyped, to be sure) that was bandied about among Presbyterian pastors.

"Daddy," he asked, "will you ever be the minister of that church?"

With the full confidence of youth, certain that my theological, ecclesiastical, and political commitments were leading in altogether different ways, I said "No, son. I probably won't be the minister of that church. I don't think they would want me."

Twenty-five years later, I am the minister of that church. The ushers no longer wear fancy coats and striped pants, and most of what I thought I knew about Fourth Presbyterian Church turned out to be false. A wonderfully diverse congregation of Christians gathers in the gothic building every week. Some are wealthy. Some are poor. Most are neither.

When I walk to the church office in the morning I see them— my congregation, my community, my parishioners if you will. I speak to Jim, the broker, and Bob, senior partner of one of the city's most prestigious law firms. I stop and chat with Carolyn on her way to Northwestern Hospital, where she works in the Hospice unit. I wave to Kim, who is a researcher for *Playboy* magazine. I give Paul a thumbs-up as he heads for the lake front on his bicycle, before resuming the search to replace the job he unexpectedly lost last week. I nod to Joe, who is walking in the garth, the church's court-yard on Michigan Avenue, an outpatient in Northwestern's drug program, homeless because his deeply painful paranoia will not let him be indoors, and so he sleeps under a bush. We are his home. He is safe here. At the door, Grace is waiting for the social service center to open. She'll have a little to eat and check in with Kevin before starting her long day on the streets, walking, pushing her grocery cart that contains all her possessions.

I'm writing this book because I love being the minister of this church. I love the human community around it, the busy, diverse, bustling, hurrying, but always human community. I love this city. I loved each congregation I have served, loved each community, each city. I need to write about that love.

But I am also writing because I think I can see something important happening in the life of the city and in the life of the church, particularly when those two lines intersect. I think that what I see here may be a paradigm, a model, for the mission and ministry of the church of Jesus Christ in the future. Intersection is the key.

Those of us who live in and care about the mainline, or old-line, or sideline churches have a lot to worry about these days. Our numbers are down. So are our financial resources. Once-viable neighborhood churches struggle with a devastating combination of deteriorating buildings, declining and aging congregations, and skyrocketing costs of everything from postage to health care for the minister. Our national structures are attacked by zealots of the left and right who, with the currently fashionable confrontational style of discourse—short on civility, long on strident melodrama—want us either to revolutionize the oppressive structures of society or to withdraw to a pious cloister foreswearing political/social movement of any kind. My own denomination, the Presbyterian Church (U.S.A.), spends an enormous amount of its energy and resources responding to, attempting to mollify, and arguing with its extremes of left and right, and it continues to watch its financial base slip.

Finally, the suburban megachurch is center stage, the subject of endless fascination and even of a four-part series in *The New York Times*, a great newspaper not inclined to give religion front-page space.

In the meantime, our best thinkers do research, analyze, evaluate, and write thoughtful tomes on our plight, such books as *American Mainline Religion*, by Wade Clark Roof and William McKinney, and *Vanishing Boundaries*, by Dean R. Hoge, Benton Johnson, and Donald A. Luidens. Other works probe the religiosity of our culture in, for instance, *A Generation of Seekers: The Spiritual Journeys of the Baby Boom Generation*, by Wade Clark Roof, and *The Culture of Disbelief: How American Law and Politics Trivialize Religious Devotion*, by Stephen L. Carter.

I have a library shelf full of books that assure me that what I am doing is irrelevant, that the future for my church is grim, that my constituency base is aging and declining, that the only religion that has a prayer these days will begin with careful market research and create user-friendly programs and ministries, even if it means dropping the tradition like a proverbial hot potato.

I read the books and I attend the seminars. I am stimulated and helped, professionally and spiritually, by the literature. Some of the authors are my friends. They are helping to save the church by forcing us to look at what we are doing very carefully. In the best tradition of academic scholarship, they force us to question all the old assumptions; not to throw up our hands in despair, but to ask simply whether God might be doing a new thing in our time, calling us to be aware of it, and asking us to join in with joy and gratitude and all the energy we can muster.

My proposal is that traditional religion, as it lives in and is expressed and celebrated by traditional churches, is important, and that in many ways the culture seems to understand, even when we don't. Traditional religion responds creatively and positively to the questions that are being asked by the culture: questions of meaning and purpose, questions of vocation and values, questions of hope.

There is about this faith of ours an internal liveliness, a constant pressure to intersect with the world. There is a radical affirmation of the world as the object of God's love and God's redemptive act in Jesus Christ, God's word made flesh. And there is the incredible confidence that this world—the city of humankind—continues to be the arena for God's gracious, redemptive activity.

When I stand in the high pulpit of Fourth Presbyterian Church on Sunday morning, take a deep breath, and look into the faces of the two thousand people who are there every Sunday of the year, I see all the people who aren't supposed to be there—busy, secular, goal-oriented, hard-working, mostly young city people. They are supposed to be home, attending to their own selfish needs or making themselves beautiful in the workout room of the Eastbank Club. Instead, they are standing as one, in the middle of the city, on what is arguably the most materialistic, aggressively secular block in America, to sing this: "Praise God from whom all blessings flow . . ." and to affirm, as one, "I believe in God the Father Almighty and in Jesus Christ . . . ."

Introduction

> Tradition is not a static thing, a great deposit of inert material like the archives of some city or university, which remains the same decade after decade, century after century. Tradition as that which the Christian past hands over to us involves not only what is handed over but also those to whom it is handed. Tradition is a living thing because its being received, if it is truly received and not just formally acknowledged, always entails discovery, surprise, nuance, interrogation and (above all) struggle.[1]
> —Douglas John Hall

I am writing this book because as the twentieth century ends, churches are in trouble. The annual decline in membership has become the norm within the old mainline churches—Presbyterian, Methodist, Episcopal, United Church of Christ—as has the decline in financial support for national church organization and mission activities. The number of parishes is also declining, as struggling congregations, both urban and rural, continue to lose numbers and support and are reluctantly and frequently painfully closed down by their parent denominations. Accompanying this, everyone agrees, is a general decline in visibility, influence, and presence of the churches in North American culture.

Those who care about the churches and seek resolutions to their dilemma, I think, often overlook one of the most important and creative resources—the tradition of the churches themselves. In fact, so eager are we to solve the problems and reverse the debilitating and humiliating decline, we are quick to abandon the tradition, even to blame the tradition for our woes.

I believe this is a mistake. I believe that the traditions of the churches may be the source of the strength and creativity we need to live faithfully into a new century; that we must be more Presbyterian, more Methodist, more Episcopal, not less. The tradition itself is lively, not moribund.

I write from the perspective of the Reformed Presbyterian tradition and out of my experience as a pastor of Presbyterian churches. I write because I love my church, and I love its affirmation of the church ecumenical, its willingness to be one part of the Holy Catholic Church and, while grounded in its own history and traditions, its willingness to appreciate, respect, and celebrate the particular history and traditions of other churches.

I write to encourage church members and leaders, laity and clergy, to find hope for the future in our traditions, to look for and discover the liveliness the past provides.

I write about my experience as pastor of a particular church, a traditional church, but in a way that I hope will be helpful to others—to pastors and people of rural and suburban, as well as urban churches.

In chapter 1 I tell the story of a city church, the Fourth Presbyterian Church of Chicago, at a particular point in time (the mid-1990s), about the culture around it, the way the church, wherever it is, is called to intersect with, converse with, and take seriously, the questions of the world, the city, and the community. Chapter 2 describes how that particular church responds to our context, our city.

Chapter 3 focuses on the people who worship and express their faith in the life of Fourth Presbyterian Church. And in chapter 4 I present three biblical characters, three seekers, as paradigms for the people who are in the pews of our churches and continue to look to the church. Chapter 5 explores the particular ways the lively tradition connects with the life of the world through the church, focusing specifically on its ministry of worship and preaching.

In chapters 6 and 7 I explore the idea that the tradition itself precipitates the church's interaction with the world along a trajectory of grace and responsibility. And in the final chapter I discuss the reasons that I have hope for the future of the churches and their lively traditions.

Those of us who love the mainline churches, who live and move and have our being in them, and who want them not only to survive but to live faithfully and strongly into the future must heed the words of the prophet addressed to another people who were anxious about the future:

Do not remember the former things,
   or consider the things of old.
I am about to do a new thing;
   now it springs forth, do you not perceive it?
                    (Isa. 43:18–19)

I believe that God has not given up on the mainline churches. I believe God will lead us and those who come after us to create new forms of the church and new structures to respond to God's grace in a new world. My hope in writing this book is that, along with our trust in God and our determination to follow our Lord faithfully, we will count among our most precious resources the traditions of the churches themselves.

I write this book in profound gratitude to the people of the four congregations I have been privileged to serve over the years, and who, with patience, forgiveness, and grace, have taught me everything I know about being a minister: the First Presbyterian Church of Dyer, Indiana; the Bethany Presbyterian Church of Lafayette, Indiana; the Broad Street Presbyterian Church of Columbus, Ohio; the Fourth Presbyterian Church of Chicago, Illinois.

I express gratitude to those who have helped with this project: Martin E. Marty, friend and mentor, who first suggested that I might have something of value to write about; Claudine Wagenaar and Judi Simon, who labored with typing and organizing; Jeanette Krenek, who coordinated this project and all the activities of my ministry; my colleagues on the staff of the Fourth Presbyterian Church of Chicago, with whom I share the privilege of ministry; and special thanks to Stephanie Egnotovich at Westminster John Knox Press, who encouraged, challenged, and helped me with professionalism and an abundance of grace.

I dedicate this modest effort to one whose grace, patience, strength, love, and faith are anything but modest: my friend, companion, and wife.

1

A Church in the City

The catholic or universal church, which is invisible, consists of the whole number of the elect, that have been, are, or shall be gathered into one, under Christ the head thereof; . . . The visible Church, which is also catholic or universal under the gospel, . . . consists of all those throughout the world that profess the true religion, together with their children; and is the Kingdom of the Lord Jesus Christ; the house and family of God . . . .
　　—The Westminster Confession of Faith, *Book of Confessions*
　　　　　　　　　　　　　　　　　XXVII, 6.140–141, PC(USA)

To be reconciled to God is to be sent into the world as his reconciling community. This community, the church universal, is entrusted with God's message of reconciliation . . . .
　　Wherever the church exists, its members are both gathered in corporate life and dispersed in society for the sake of mission in the world.
　　—The Confession of 1967, *Book of Confessions* 9.31, 9.35,
　　　　　　　　　　　　　　　　　　　　　　　PC(USA)

The causes for the change are vast and complex, but they are linked to the massive urbanization of the world that has occurred in this century. The great dislocation and uprooting that this seismic shift entails have had at least two results. They have cut the nerve of traditional religion which is often tied to specific geographical locations and cultural patterns. . . . The culture shock caused by this harrowing trek to the big city has pushed these pioneers into a search for new forms of community and an effort to retrieve and transform old symbols and beliefs.[1]
　　　　　　　　　　　　　　　　　　　　　　—Harvey Cox

"God so loved the world." That's where it begins for us. Our faith and trust in God, our commitment to Jesus Christ, our belonging to the community of faith, the people of God, the church—all rest on the firm foundation of God's love for the world. The human community is the object: the city, the town, the neighborhood where we find ourselves.

Sometimes we Christians have seemed not to believe the basic affirmation of God's love for the human community. Sometimes we have seemed to mistrust the world. Sometimes we have seemed suspicious of the city in particular, entertaining the notion, which is hardly new, that the city is an inherently evil place.

But God loves the world. And the church, God's people, lives in the world God loves, is part of the world God loves, and is part of the world for which God's son lived and died.

In the summer of 1995, two events occurred in Chicago that define something of what modern American life has become and also demonstrate why the health and vitality, in fact, the very existence of the churches, is a matter of importance for our society, our cities, and communities, not to mention the churches themselves. Everyone knew about the first event. The only people who knew about the second event were the ministers, staff, and a few members and friends of the Fourth Presbyterian Church of Chicago.

On Thursday, July 13, the temperature at O'Hare Airport reached 106 degrees, the hottest day in Chicago since official records have been kept. The residents of lake-front highrises and brownstones stayed indoors. In Lake Forest and Deerfield people prayed that the demands on the electrical supply to power hundreds of thousands of air conditioners would not exceed the utility's ability to generate it. In the Chicago Housing Authority's apartments, people opened windows, slept on bare floors, or sat outside all night, waiting for a blessed breath of moving air.

By Friday, something unexpected, new, and tragic started to happen. The elderly, the sick, the people who live alone, the ones who double and triple lock windows and doors, and who live in such fear of violent crime that they venture outside only when necessary, began to die. Before the worst heat wave in history broke, more than six hundred Chicagoans had died of heat-related causes, and the city was stunned. Who was to blame? city government? the mayor? a communications system that failed to get word of city cooling centers out quickly enough? Or did the welfare system fail? Some people even tried to blame the victims themselves for not understanding the threat the heat posed and asking for help from neighbors. The physicians went to work to explain how deadly intense heat can be. Someone must be at fault. How could it happen that hundreds of people died of heat in a major American city, "The City that Works," in the Year of our Lord 1995?

And then it began to dawn on us that the tragedy occurred because something has happened to the notion of community in our land. Vulnerable, elderly, fragile people died because no one knew about their vulnerability and fragility. No one cared. No one knew they existed.

We're still thinking about it, those of us who live in Chicago, but so are people in other cities and towns and villages where the sense of community, the everyday reality of neighbors caring for one another, seems to be receding and disappearing. Those of us who belong to churches, who lead churches, who live out our lives as the church were reminded, tragically, of the great gift of the church and that the vitality and health and very existence of churches is a matter of life and death.

Churches enhance, celebrate, and sometimes give life simply by reason of being communities in which people know and care about one another. During the heat wave, The Caring Connection at Fourth Presbyterian Church and similar programs at hundreds of other churches were operating. Church members were telephoning the elderly and the shut-ins and, as necessary, performing small acts of caring that were life-saving. The heat wave of 1995 reminded me that the health of the churches is a very important matter.

The second event in the hot summer of 1995 in Chicago was a memorial service, conducted by an associate pastor of Fourth Presbyterian Church and attended by a handful of other church staff members and a few social workers. This event was not covered by the media. In fact, it went unnoticed by everyone but those who attended—few in number but a small community of support, compassion, and love for the person who had died.

Mary Wojac was her name, a fifty-five-year-old woman with no family who had spent most of the last ten years on the streets of Chicago. Mary was not exactly homeless. Through the efforts of devoted and determined social workers, she had an apartment. But Mary was, the social workers told me, a paranoid schizophrenic. Her episodes were frequent and severe. In her paranoic state she could not be inside any enclosure; she could not be indoors and would not return to her apartment; in fact, she lost track of the fact that she had an apartment. During her episodes, Mary would scavenge for food in the trash cans and dumpsters behind the North Side's wonderful restaurants and walk the streets, head down, smoking cigarette after cigarette, speaking to no one, seeing no one. In her frequent paranoid episodes, Fourth Presbyterian Church became her anchor and, increasingly, her home. All day long she sat on first one entry stair and then another, moving occasionally to the stone benches in front of the church building on Michigan Avenue. The only person she would talk to was the director of the church's social service center, Kevin Olson. Occasionally Kevin could persuade Mary to return to her apartment. Sometimes he succeeded in convincing her to come inside the church to The Door, our social service center, for a bowl of soup and to use the restroom. Often Kevin, or one of his staff, brought her a sandwich and a jacket or a blanket, and Mary would spend the night somewhere outside the church building, huddled for warmth and safety beneath its gray stone walls.

Even in the mysterious depths of her psychosis, Mary knew us. When, the summer before, during extensive renovation, the church offices and programs moved a block away to an empty office building, Mary came along, continuing what was for her an anchoring and life-sustaining connection. As it happened, our temporary quarters were directly across the street from one of Chicago's oldest and most elite private clubs that had an elegant marquis protecting its entrance from the elements—a perfect place to be on one of Chicago's bitterly cold and gusty winter days. Sometimes Mary, who had followed us to our new quarters, walked across the street and spread her blanket on the doorstep of the exclusive club under the protection of the elegant marquis for an afternoon nap or for the night. And sometimes the members of the club, arriving for lunch or cocktail hour, had to gingerly and carefully step over Mary, enjoying her nap. Never did they force her to leave. And always, when I observed it, I smiled in the assurance that God was smiling and that something of the essential nature of the church of God was being expressed. When Mary died of the chronic heart condition her hard life had exacerbated, she was not alone. The memorial service celebrating her life, thanking God for the gift of her life, was the church of Jesus Christ bearing its most eloquent witness.

It is an interesting time to be the church in this city, or anywhere in this country, for that matter. Many of us were born and came of age in a very different era. My hometown, Altoona, Pennsylvania, a small industrial city situated at the foot of the Allegheny Mountains' steepest ascent, was settled by European immigrants who followed the railroad west. Their churches are reminders of a time when communities were formed on the basis of ethnicity, language, and religion; Mount Carmel, St. Mary's, Immaculate Conception, and on our side of town, literally divided in half by the tracks of the Pennsylvania Railroad's mainline, First Methodist, First Lutheran, and the Broad Avenue Presbyterian Church, my faith community. On the highest hill in the middle of the city, visible from all directions, stood the Cathedral of the Blessed Sacrament, with a towering dome, majestic portals flanked by broad stone steps, and a mystically dark interior adorned with statues and frescoes. It was, and is, the tallest building in the city. To come of age in that place and time was to know, even if you did not belong to or attend one of those neighborhood churches or the magnificent cathedral, that there was a certain rhythm to life. God was in heaven. And all was, if not well, at least orderly, in the world.

The Marginalization of the Church

In the narrow band of American experience that is my lifetime, a revolution has happened. The older order of things is gone. Its disappearance is part of a bigger picture of cultural change, of course. Things change in the broader sweep of history. Paradigms shift, to use the currently fashionable phrase. The first time I saw a European cathedral I recognized the scene, and the order, immediately. The spires of Salisbury Cathedral are visible from miles away. The medieval cathedral towered over the entire community and surrounding countryside. Its bells marked the hours. Its square was filled daily with the noisy urban activity of commerce, entertainment, festival, and socialization.

Today, modern American city churches, where they still exist, live in a very different order. Trinity Episcopal Church, at the foot of Wall Street, the richest church in America, appears to be tiny in contrast to the canyon of skyscrapers all around it.

When we published a history of the Fourth Presbyterian Church, *A Light in the City*, Marilee Munger Scroggs, the author, and Micah Marty, the photographer, included four photographs of Chicago's North Michigan Avenue taken from the same spot but at intervals of twenty years. In 1923, the gray gothic building of Fourth Presbyterian Church is one of the largest, substantial, and most visible structures in the neighborhood. By 1990, the church has virtually disappeared from sight. One of my favorite views of the church I serve as pastor is from the top of the John Hancock Center, directly across the street, ninety-six stories high. From the observation tower, the church appears small, dwarfed by tall buildings on all sides.

Some suggest that this spatial relationship, the relative diminish-
ment of the church in the modern American city is a symbol of what
is happening to religion in general, and Christian faith in particular,
in our culture. Beneath the feverish concern about the decline of the
mainline churches is the more critical concern about the place and
relevance of traditional religious faith in modern life. The issue is
not simply how to keep the Methodist and Episcopal and
Presbyterian churches alive; the issue is how to be faithful, how to
speak about God and faith intelligently and honestly, how to live
with integrity and faith in a new world no one has ever seen or experienced before.

Harvard theologian Harvey Cox argues that while the city did
not turn out to be as secular as everybody thought it was, traditional
religion and traditional churches are more and more squeezed out,
marginalized, forced to exist in the corners or niches of city culture.

If it is true that the cathedral defined medieval culture and that
the white-frame church, with its steeple blessing the rolling hills of
New England or the awesome expanse of midwestern prairie,
defined the life of American culture for two centuries, the structure
that best represents modernity and the modern city, Cox maintains,
is the airport. And, he observes, religion is a very marginal activity
at the airport. And I wonder, Where is God? Where is religion?
There are niches at Logan and O'Hare and elsewhere, airport
chapels, squeezed into a corner in a remote corner of the complex.

The point is not that religion ought to play a more visible role in
modern airports. In fact, it seems to me that there is probably more
praying and invoking the Lord's name, although not always in rev-
erence, in airports and airplanes than most places. On a flight
recently, our plane hit a sudden, unexpected pocket and dropped
what felt like several hundred feet. Cups and glasses and ice cubes
flew, the woman across the aisle, with whom I had been talking
about church, exclaimed automatically, "Jesus Christ!" It wasn't
profanity, I concluded. It was a most appropriate prayer of petition
under the circumstances, although she looked sheepish when we
leveled and stabilized and apologized profusely and incessantly.

The point is that traditional religion and traditional churches
are squeezed out of the culture and pushed into out-of-the-way
corners by modern American life. And part of what is happening
as the traditional churches continue to decline is that religion itself
is marginalized.

My first exposure to the marginalization of religion in the culture
was harsh, and I still experience the sting, years after the fact,

although I can now laugh about the incident. I arrived in Hyde Park to begin my graduate work at the Divinity School of the University of Chicago and Chicago Theological Seminary in 1959. I was young, intellectually naive, and spiritually untried. I had come to the Divinity School because a wise college advisor told me it was a good place to ask the kinds of questions I was asking, that the faculty and administration wouldn't push me into making a decision about a vocation as a minister, and that Chicago Theological Seminary and the University of Chicago were generous with scholarship and fellowship money. He was correct in all three descriptions. But I arrived in Hyde Park without much by way of theological experience.

It wasn't long before I learned three new names: Paul Tillich, Reinhold Niebuhr, and Karl Barth. Most of the people I met at the University of Chicago liked to describe themselves as "Tillichians." I was impressed. I had never heard of the man, and here were bright, earnest classmates using his name to define themselves! A few claimed to be "Niebuhrians." Nobody was a "Barthian." In fact, everybody seemed to be angry with Barth, even though his son Markus taught New Testament on the Divinity School faculty. I decided it was important to be something: a Tillichian, Niebuhrian, a Barthian. So I ventured to Fifty-seventh Street and stopped in the first bookstore I encountered. It was small—a little disorganized it seemed. I was unable to find a single volume by any of my three authors.

Thelonius Monk (at least I knew *his* name) was improvising in the background; a balding, bearded man sat behind the counter smoking something that smelled sweet and musty. He was reading a book of poetry. He did not acknowledge my presence.

"Can you help me?" I asked. "I'm looking for something by Paul Tillich, or Reinhold Niebuhr, or Karl Barth."

He placed the book of poetry carefully on the counter, looked at me incredulously and said, with startling passion, "Why the hell do you want to read that garbage!"

I stammered something about being a new student at the divinity school.

"That figures," he observed with noticeable disdain, and picked up the poetry book again.

On a recent visit to Athens, I found myself, comparing with appropriate modesty I hope, that still-vivid rebuke to, of all things, St. Paul's experience at the Acropolis.

Athens, the crown jewel of human civilization, had seen better days by the time Paul visited in A.D. 50. Socrates had died four hundred fifty years earlier; the political center of civilization had moved west to Rome; and the greatest seaport and commercial center of the region was down the coast at Corinth. What Athens still excelled at was sophistication, urbanity. The whole city must have been like Hyde Park, where Nobel Prize-winning economists walk the sidewalks and sip cappuccino with nuclear physicists, sociologists, and even theologians; where dialogue is intense, incessant, exhausting, and always confrontational.

Athens was famous for that. Leaders and teachers of the two predominant schools of philosophy, the Stoics and the Epicureans, established themselves there. There was a university and a kind of intellectual tribunal to determine the viability of new ideas. And there was a place, the Areopagus, a hill with a rocky outcrop at the top where the philosophers went every day to engage one another in conversation and where others came to listen, learn, and be amused.

When he came to Athens, Paul was taken to the Areopagus and given a hearing. The philosophers had heard about him and his strange new ideas, and they wanted to engage him in dialogue.

What Paul said in Athens is significantly different from the content and method of his speeches elsewhere, as the New Testament describes it. It appears that he knew enough about the philosophers and their schools of thought to borrow their methods of public discourse and even to quote an anonymous poet in his allusion to God as one "in him we live and move and have our being" (Acts 17:28).

Paul acknowledged the Athenian interest in religion, complimented them on their altar to "the unknown God." God, the Athenians and the philosophers agreed, is known in creation—God, the maker of all things, God the "first cause." As they nodded in approval, Paul made his theological and homiletical move—this God we all acknowledge as creator, this one in whom we live and move and have being, this God raised his "appointed man," Jesus of Nazareth, from the dead. There must have been a thunderous silence. "Did he say what we think we heard him say?" they must have asked. "How did he get from the lovely abstractions we enjoy discussing to death and resurrection?"

They scoffed, Luke reports. Some showed a little interest, but not many, and Paul left. Interestingly, not only was he not very successful there, at least not noticeably at first, but Athens was the only place where Paul presented the claims of the gospel that he did not stir up some kind of resistance and persecution.

This is what happens to Christian faith in a big city, I believe. It is pushed aside, marginalized, by a sophisticated intellectualism that enjoys the rigor of a good argument but is not willing to be committed, to believe, trust, live, and die for faith. And perhaps that is what is happening to the churches, particularly city churches, but in a sense all the churches in our culture, overwhelmed by the sheer size and muscularity of the institutions around them, dwarfed and diminished by commerce, power, and the speed, frenzy, and complexity of modern life.

The Resurgence of Religion

But at the same time the churches are marginalized, people are asking religious questions with new urgency. Questions of value, meaning, hope, and the human prospect are, in one way or another, addressed in many of the books people are reading, the theater they are attending, the motion pictures they are watching. "Chant," a compact disc recording of the Benedictine monks of the monastery of Santo Domingo de Silos in Spain, sold tens of thousands of copies, and the monks are on the charts again with a new recording of Gregorian chants. Gregorian chant—living comfortably, competitively, and successfully with gangsta rap and hard rock and a new market!

Harvey Cox, again in a new book on Pentecostalism, joins his voice with many others in observing that there is a hunger for authentic religion in our culture, a religion of heart as well as mind, a religiosity that feels as well as thinks, and is unapologetically public about its expression and its moral implications. Cox maintains that while mainline religion is declining, Pentecostalism "has succeeded because it has spoken to the spiritual emptiness of our time by reaching beyond the levels of creed and ceremony into the core of human religiousness, into what might be called 'primal spirituality,' that largely unprocessed nucleus of the psyche in which the unending struggle for a sense of purpose and significance goes on."[2]

At the very time the human enterprise revels in its rationalism and objective scientific reason as arbiter of all truth, a primal spirituality that welcomes mystical and personal religious experience is reappearing. Something like 80 percent of the American people confess, confidentially, to having had a personal religious experience. And once again, thousands of the faithful, or curious, or a combination of faithful and curious, are flocking to witness the latest weeping Madonna fresco on the transept wall of a Ukrainian Orthodox Cathedral in Chicago.

We modern, urban Americans are, as Paul described the people of Athens two thousand years ago, "extremely religious in every way." We may have witnessed the marginalization of traditional religion, but we are wide awake spiritually and open to new expressions, new forms, new ways of being religious.

I will describe them more fully in a subsequent chapter, but the people I look out on from the pulpit of Fourth Presbyterian Church on Sunday morning are what Wade Clark Roof calls a "generation of seekers," asking religious questions, looking for authentic religious experience.

It's not an entirely new phenomenon, of course. The ancient psalmist wrote:

> O God, you are my God, I seek you,
>   my soul thirsts for you;
> my flesh faints for you,
>   as in a dry and weary land where there is no water.
>   (Psalm 63:1)

So, is there not reason for a not-so-cautious optimism about the future of religion and the churches? Is there not reason to trust that the gospel we believe is God's answer to this new questioning, God's living water for our thirst, and bread for our hunger? Is there not a compelling reason to look again at our own precious theological and ecclesiastical traditions as a source for a lively and authentic renewal of faith and to hope for, and expect, a reemergence of the church as a vitally healthy presence in the midst of modern life? With everything in me, I believe there is.

In *American Congregations*, edited by James Wind and James Lewis, Langdon Gilkey has written an essay, "The Christian Congregations as a Religious Community." Gilkey's point is so simple, so essential, that its truth frequently eludes us, I fear. He argues that congregations are effective to the degree that they are "religious." While most current emphasis is on community, the critical matter for those of us who care about and lead churches is how a congregation is "a religious entity, or, in special Christian language, how it is that God, or God's grace acts in, is present to, or empowers the community."[3]

We are not as secular as we thought we were. The old religious questions—questions of meaning and purpose, life and death, guilt and grace, and above all, hope—are very much with us. My sense is that to the degree churches know the questions, acknowledge the questions, help formulate the questions, live thoroughly in the world that is generating the questions, enter into rigorous and honest dialogue with the questions—to the degree that churches are authentically religious entities entering into dialogue with the authentically religious questions modern men and women are asking, they will be faithful, healthy and, in all probability, full of people every time their doors are open.

Paul identified with the city's intellectual and spiritual quest: "Athenians, I see how extremely religious you are in every way. For as I went through the city and looked carefully at the objects of your worship, I found among them an altar with the inscription, 'To an unknown God'" (Acts 17:22–23).

Paul's strategy was, first, to identify with and affirm the authenticity of the city and the city's quest. We must do the same, wherever God calls us to be the church. "Chicagoans . . . New Yorkers . . . Los Angelinos . . . and everybody in between, I see how extremely religious you are in every way."

Our first strategy must be to embrace the city, whatever human community is our locus, our home. Before we do or say anything, the churches need to affirm and celebrate what is good, creative, and hopeful about the city, that is about the human community. We haven't always done that. To the contrary, the churches sometimes—often, in fact—have spoken and acted in ways that are suspicious of the city, have regarded the city as inherently dangerous and evil and confirmed the old stereotypes of the city as a morally corrupt source of vice and sin.

This attitude toward the city is not new. As a city minister who works and resides, "lives, moves, and has being" in the heart of the city, I loved learning about the superstition in Jesus' day that demons and evil spirits that had been cast out of a person's body did not roam aimlessly around the countryside, but headed instead directly for the city.

So Where Exactly Is God?

There is, and always has been since the Hebrews looked longingly at the natural religion of their new neighbors in the land of Canaan, the sense that God is more accessible to us in nature than in the ambiguity of human community or the messiness of human history and experience.

A suspicion has always existed that if you want to be in touch with God, you must escape from the noise, dirt, and clutter of the city and retreat to the mountains, country, lakeside, or seashore.

The goodness and holiness of creation are strong theological and biblical themes and are the faith tradition's built-in corrective to Christianity's otherworldly tilt God created. God likes what God created. Creation is good. My earliest experience of the mysterious presence of what I later learned to call the Holy, the "Numen," the "mysterium tremendum" occured while I was lying on my back looking directly up into the full, green canopy of a grove of pine trees. I was ten or eleven years old, a first-year junior camper at the Presbytery of Huntington's summer conference center, Camp Shekinah. It was an old Civilian Conservation Corps work camp, long abandoned, and to say the least, it lacked amenities: elongated barracks for fifty bunks with a single cold water spigot outside.

Can you imagine fifty eleven-year-old boys living for a week in that? Can you imagine the courage and devotion of the adult counselors who consented to give a week of their summer vacation to live with us like that? What Camp Shekinah lacked by way of human comfort it more than made up for in natural beauty. The mountains that surrounded the campsite were lush and thickly forested. The site itself had been carefully and systematically planted with pine trees along every walk, around every open space. The ground was soft with accumulated needles. The color everywhere was pine green, and in the air was the beautiful and compelling aroma of a pine forest.

And so I met the God of creation. Years later, struggling over Karl Barth's passionate argument with Emil Brunner about natural theology (Barth had bluntly and with absolute confidence utterly rejected Brunner's suggestion that something of God can be known in the natural world, the creation, in an essay he characteristically titled "Nein"), I kept thinking about Camp Shekinah.

After breakfast the regimen called for each of the campers to take a Bible and the daily devotional guide the leadership had distributed, find a quiet spot, and sit and read and pray. The rule was absolute silence. No one spoke throughout the camp. Even the cooks and kitchen KPs ceased their clean-up activities so as not to disrupt the silence. We sat with backs against a tree, or on the occasional bench, wherever we could find a spot. Mine was in a small grove of towering pine trees. I don't recall what I read or prayed or even whether I followed the instructions at all. What I recall, as if it were yesterday, was one day lying on my back and seeing the most magnificent sight I had ever witnessed—that glorious canopy of pine, with refracted rays of sun shining through, and the soft needles beneath my back, and the smell——. At that moment something of the mystery and grandeur and presence of the creator God was given to me.

After dinner the entire camp walked a half mile or so to Vesper Hill. When we arrived at the path that led up the short distance to a clearing where there were rows of low, log benches and a rough wood pulpit and cross, the silence rule was invoked again. No talking on Vesper Hill. When we assembled, the camp choir, mostly girls I recall, worked its way through the introit whose melody replays in my memory:

The Lord is in his holy temple
Let all the earth keep silence before him.
Keep silence, keep silence,
Keep silence, keep silence.

I made the connection. That place, Vesper Hill, Camp Shekinah, was the holy temple of God. The mountains and setting sun, the pine trees and soft pine needle carpet, the aroma—God's holy temple. And I continue to experience the connection.

I do not live close to nature most of the time. Most of us do not. Nor have I ever been as disciplined and persistent in daily devotions as I have aspired to be. My praying is mostly on the run, in bits and pieces, here and there throughout too-busy days of activity. But there are occasions and places, enough of them to sustain me, when I can and do read, think, reflect, pray, write about God and to God. One such place is on the screened-in porch of a small house Sue and I bought on two wooded acres in southern Michigan, with the sun rising and the mist lifting from the pale green meadow and the birds creating a chorus of brilliance and beauty. Or when we make our annual pilgrimage to the ocean and I, rising early, find a spot to do my devotions as I did at Camp Shekinah, and know this once again in the very depths of my soul:

The earth is the Lord's and all that is in it,
    the world, and those who live in it;
for he has founded it on the seas,
    and established it on the rivers.
            (Psalm 24:1–2)

But that is only a part of the truth and, over the years, only part of my experience. Even though I argued with Karl Barth's almost arrogant dismissal of Emil Brunner's natural theology and, by extension, my precious Camp Shekinah experience, not to mention the lovely early-morning devotionals on the screened-in porch or at the ocean, I have concluded, and regularly conclude, that Barth was at least half right. There is more to the faith than natural theology. There is something absolutely critical about the gospel of Jesus Christ that is incarnational, worldly, focused on and in the ambiguity and complexity of the human experience, the human community, the human city.

And again, it came to me in an experience that I recall with as much detailed clarity as Camp Shekinah. The context, however, could not be more dissimilar. I was a seminary student, serving a small congregation in Dyer, Indiana, as part-time student and pastor. Sue and I were expecting our second child that summer. I decided to take advantage of the fact that we would not be traveling away from home for vacation to earn some desperately needed extra money. A friend and neighbor arranged for me to be hired by the Ford Motor Company at its huge Chicago Heights stamping plant. "You'll have to be a production worker," she said, apologizing for not being able to get me a job in the office. Actually, I liked the idea. Production workers were at the bottom of the labor force hierarchy. But the pay was handsome, particularly compared with a student pastor's stipend.

I worked the day shift, 7:00 A.M. to 3:30 P.M., thirty minutes for lunch, with two twelve-minute breaks during the day. I operated welding machines, pushed automobile hoods, roofs, doors, along the line from the big stamping presses to the next station when various parts were fastened, adjustments made, refinements performed. It was good work, for many reasons: physically hard, but mentally numbing. The challenge for me was to avoid a kind of deadening, almost narcotic, boredom.

I drove from our quiet house in the early morning, parked in the immense lot, climbed the stairs to the entry point, walked with hundreds of others coming and going through security through several sets of doors and into the largest space I had ever seen, the most visually and aurally violent I have ever experienced. The noise from the stamping presses was deafening. Sparks flew from the thousands of welding stations, machinery whined, forklifts roared: human conversation happened only at a full-volume shout. It was bright, loud, and hot. And for some reason, one day, when I entered that space I found myself, unaccountably, singing to myself,

The Lord is in his holy temple,
Let all the earth keep silence before him

The Camp Shekinah Vesper Hill choral introit in, of all places, a noisy, dirty, hot automobile factory! I have never forgotten that day, that experience. The hair on the back of my neck stood up, and a lump came to my throat. I'm not sure it was that day I became a Christian, but I know that an important and ultimately critically formative part of my theology, my spirituality, fell into place. It was the day I learned about and experienced incarnation.

The Chicago Heights Ford stamping plant is the holy temple of God, every bit as authentically as was Vesper Hill at Camp Shekinah. Nature and history. Creation and community. The earth is the Lord's, and so is the human experience, the human city.

So Where Exactly Is the Church?

The church, I believe, is a respite of silence from the noise of the city; a cloistered, reflective place where mystery and transcendence may be pondered, where prayers are lifted in solitude. But if that is all church is, an escape, a retreat from the world, it has made a critical mistake. The church is called to be in the world, in the city, and that means intentionally, imaginatively, creatively, and aggressively in the city, living in and for the human community in order to be faithful to God.

Professor Langdon Gilkey writes this:

> The secular world as a fallen world—and that it surely is—calls for a religious community of grace . . . just as the secular world as a wonderful creation of intelligence, moral responsibility, political liberation, and technical skill calls for a liberal religious community devoted to accommodation to the world's creativity. How to balance these two requirements is a trick practiced with accomplishment only in the kingdom.[4]

Well, maybe. But we ought to be trying. One thing is certain—this city, Chicago, is a sheer wonder. Those of us privileged to live in it know that it is impossible to be bored by it. The Fourth Church morning choir participated in the Salzburg, Austria, Church Music Festival. The choir sang beautifully in Salzburg's magnificent Dom and while in Austria at the Capuchin church in Vienna, and memorably for all who experienced it, stopped to sing "Virga Jesse" in St.

Florian Abbey, Anton Bruckner's burial place. It was a glorious experience. But after a week or so I became aware of the racial homogeneity of the place. It didn't feel right. On the day we arrived home in Chicago, my wife and I walked north along the lake front through Lincoln Park, adjacent to the zoo. We walked past and through the late afternoon leisure activity of the people of Chicago: African-American couples strolling, children from the projects playing and running, Anglo Saxon yuppies riding ten-speed trail bikes. The cooking odors from the array of portable grills punctuated the magnificent cultural diversity of this country and this city, particularly. We have work to do; plenty of it. We are divided, segregated, alienated socially and racially. But a thirty-minute walk along the lake in Chicago does provide a picture of the human community something akin to what God must have in mind.

A city is a racial/ethnic kaleidoscope, replete with customs, languages, costumes, skin colors, music, and food that we are privileged to experience and that I miss when it is not present.

Our city is a wonder. Its art and music are among the best in the world. Where else can you visit the most extensive collection of French Impressionist paintings in the world, free of charge on Tuesdays? Where else can you hear one of the finest musical organizations in the world, the Chicago Symphony Orchestra or the distinguished Grant Park Symphony Orchestra, free, under the stars?

Within the city, an integral part of the community, are universities, contributing to the spirit of the metropolitan area: research teaching hospitals; four major league professional teams that add enormously to the liveliness, joy, and sometimes grief of the community.

The churches are part of all that the modern city is. It is important to find ways to express that, to give visible form to our incarnational theology; not simply accommodating ourselves to the city and its values, but affirming with joy and commitment that the city is a particularly intense and critical part of the creation God loves. Each church can decide how best to express that, but my deep conviction is that the expression of commitment to and involvement in the life of the community is the foundation of any appropriate urban witness and mission.

One of the ways affirmation and celebration of the community/city/world happens in the life of Fourth Presbyterian Church is the annual Festival of the Arts. The purpose of the festival is to celebrate the traditional and honorable relationship between religion and the arts and to remind the city, as imaginatively as we can, that religion and the arts are often up to the same things—trying to find ways to express the mystery of God, trying through the beauty of holiness and the occasional holiness of beauty to praise the God of creation and creativity. It is not an occasion to display paintings of exclusively traditional religious subjects or to invite the neighbors in for an old-fashioned hymn sing.

One year we commissioned a Milwaukee artist, Marian Vieux, to do a series of what she calls her "tree sculptures," using the trees that border our buildings along Michigan Avenue and Chestnut Street and grace the "garth," our peculiar word for courtyard. Marian's mode of sculpture is tree wrapping. For several days she and her associates wrapped the trunks and branches with brightly colored strips of plastic, alternating yellow and blue and pink and green. One tree was wrapped in scarlet, every branch. The effect of her work was to show us trees for the first time. Jesus stopped his listeners in their tracks one time with the simple admonition, "Consider the lilies." Marian stopped thousands of Chicagoans hustling up and down Michigan Avenue with her lively, brilliant art that said simply and eloquently, "Consider the trees."

In other years we have featured a variety of imaginatively creative benches for passersby to try, a series of enormous metal "urban musical instruments" that visitors to our garth could pluck, rattle, or hammer to make oddly lovely urban music and, on one memorable occasion, a huge sail attached to the base of our steeple and grounded in the stalwart stone cloister. The artist assured us, wrongly as it turned out, that he had engineered the work precisely to accommodate Chicago's legendary wind. When the sail began to loosen the mortar on the steeple, the trustees decided that art would be temporarily sacrificed for safety.

We have exhibited Chicago photographers, painters, and sculptors on religious and nonreligious themes. And we have invited guest performers, lecturers, poets, and conductors to participate. We have sold tickets to our members, friends, and neighbors, always providing free or reduced admission to those unable to pay, and we have mostly broken even. Maya Angelou has read and lectured, Robert Shaw has conducted, Dave Brubeck has played and conducted performances of his sacred music, on two occasions, and Paul Winter, jazz saxophonist and artist in residence at New York's Cathedral of St. John the Divine, has brought the Paul Winter Consort to Fourth Church on three occasions for evenings of lively traditional and nontraditional jazz, folk, new age, and ethnic music, as well as Winter's popular specialty, the music of whales and wolves. It is a wonderful moment when in the darkened gothic sanctuary of Fourth Presbyterian Church, Winter invites his audience to shed self-consciousness, and with heads tilted back and eyes shut, howl like the wolves—and we do it! A "Howl-lelujah Chorus," Paul Winter calls it.

Not every church can do it this way, but every church can do something to affirm and celebrate its community, the world around it, to say as eloquently and imaginatively as possible that the human community is a wonder, that God loves the human community, that God's son came into it, demonstrating God's love, to redeem and save it.

The Church's Challenge

In the introduction to a new book on the Apostles' Creed, *Credo*, Roman Catholic theologian Hans Küng proposes that in order to communicate what it believes, the church must always understand the questions people are asking. "Taking seriously the questions of contemporaries," he calls it, and by that he means that we must always listen carefully to what the world, the people around us, the particular men, women, and children who walk past the churches every day, are asking, saying, thinking, and feeling.[5]

"Let the world set the agenda," we used to say in the sixties. I do not mean that at all. The agenda has already been set for us. It is the gospel of Jesus Christ: to believe it, proclaim it, and live it out in the world as congregations, as faithfully as we are able. We already have an agenda, but if we do not understand what people are asking, our answers, our preachments, programs, and projects will be irrelevant. It is not a bad idea for church leaders and planners to keep close at hand that now-famous subway graffiti—"Christ is the answer," under which someone else had written simply, eloquently, "What's the question?"

The pastor is responsible for knowing the questions and for understanding, explaining, interpreting the culture with as much disciplined thoughtfulness as she or he works at the lectionary texts for each Sunday's sermon. A friend of mine who teaches homiletics wanted to test his thesis that most current preaching is not related to what is actually happening in the world and, therefore, is unrelated to what is in the minds and hearts of the particular people sitting in the pews waiting for the sermon on Sunday morning. The week after American bombs began to drop on Iraqi forces in Kuwait, he and his assistants telephoned a randomly selected number of churches around the country and asked whether the preacher had said anything about the fact that the nation was engaged in very serious military activity, that casualties had happened and were about to increase? He was not looking for ideological/political responses to the particular decision national leaders were making but was trying to discover whether or not the most important fact of life for the American people on that particular Sunday had found its way into the sermon, or the prayers, or even the announcements. He discovered that in the vast majority of the churches contacted, it had not. No mention was made of the initiation of serious military action by American forces anywhere in the Sunday morning worship experience.

Marginalization happens when the churches do not hear the questions people are asking, when churches do not live thoroughly in the world and therefore do not know what is in the hearts and spirits of people who do live thoroughly in the world.

The church is called to be in the world, perhaps not "of" the world, but most certainly "in" it, without reservation or apology. It is an incarnational expression for us. Just as Jesus Christ is God's commitment to the world, God's life lived out in the world, so the church, the Body of Christ lives thoroughly and without reservation in the world, not abstractly, but in the city, the community, the particular neighborhood.

Part of the responsibility of the Evangelism Committee at Fourth Presbyterian Church is to keep an ear open for the questions the people of the city are asking and to determine whether it might be useful for the church to become an intentional part of the conversation, not so much by providing answers to the questions—churches try to do that too much already, mostly ineffectively, by the way—but by being part of the dialogue or by enabling the dialogue to occur publicly. It is an Evangelism Committee responsibility, not mission or social action, because we believe that effective communication of the gospel will not happen until people have some sense that the evangelist knows what questions they are asking.

The programmatic shape it takes at Fourth Presbyterian Church is something we call the Michigan Avenue Forum. Occasionally, in response to an event, a controversial topic, a question people are asking, we present a forum: midday, evening, or Saturday morning, depending on the targeted participants.

When the movie *The Last Temptation of Christ*, Martin Scorcese's version of Nicholas Kazauzakus's provocative novel, was released and some churches were protesting, condemning the movie for blasphemy and scandal, even picketing the theaters where the movie was being shown, and many thoughtful people weren't sure whether to be angry or intrigued, we held a Michigan Avenue Forum on the topic. We put a phone call into Scorcese himself to participate, but he wasn't available. We did manage to get Richard Ostling, religious editor for *TIME* Magazine, and Robert Jewett, who teaches New Testament at Garrett-Evangelical Seminary; we put out a sign announcing it and one afternoon at noon had a Michigan Avenue Forum on *The Last Temptation of Christ* that was very useful.

Other forums have focused on the question of euthanasia, on public education, on a countywide election that was polarizing the city along racial lines (the candidates were pleased to be invited, and most participated) on casino gambling, which the Mayor says we must have for our city's long-term fiscal viability but which most of the churches and many of the city's institutions oppose. Our most recent forum was on the topic of violence and guns. A top juvenile officer from the Chicago Police Department made a passionate presentation. An urban sociologist and public school official also participated, and our sanctuary was half full on a Saturday morning.

Taking the questions seriously is the beginning of evangelism. The Michigan Avenue Forums tell the people of the city, even if they do not actually attend a forum, that the church is in the city. Every church can and must find a way to express that critical, incarnational commitment to our community.

We live in a critical time for the churches. Enormous and significant cultural change has occurred in the religious situation making it very different from what many of us experienced in the past. Our churches have declined numerically and also in terms of public influence. In many American cities and communities, once thriving congregations have seen membership decline, buildings age and become more demanding to maintain, budgets tighten, and mission reduced to institutional survival.

The traditional churches appear to be in a lot of trouble in our nation and in our cities. And yet the American people are asking religious questions—questions of value, meaning, purpose, and hope—as never before.

The challenge is for the churches to understand the importance and the power of this new spirituality, this new quest for authentic religion. The challenge is for the churches to understand the questions, to listen to the city, to enter into the dialogue that is going on in the arts, literature, entertainment. It begins, I believe, with a deeply spiritual commitment to love the world and the city, to live thoroughly in the world and city, to know profoundly that God's good creation includes the city and that God is mysteriously but always lovingly and redemptively present in the life of the city.

Those of us who care about the church and who pray and work for the renewal of the church must help the church in the demanding task of listening to the world, and then in the equally demanding task of responding faithfully. Sometimes we will create programs that respond immediately and directly to the world's questions and needs. And sometimes being a faithful church will mean participating in the conversation, sharing the world's hurt, hopes, and fears. Sometimes churches can lead. Sometimes churches should follow. Always churches must live unapologetically and thoroughly in the world, in the midst of the human community where God calls us to be.

It is a critical time, and we have a word to say, we have love to share, and we have a saving gospel to live. In a time of social dislocation and alienation, we know about community. In a time when people die alone in the midst of a heat wave, we know about a tie that binds us to one another and calls us to love and care for one another. We know about grace and hope. Because our tradition places us thoroughly in the midst of the human community, I believe there are reasons to believe that our future will be lively and hopeful.

2

The Church's Mission

The great ends of the Church are the proclamation of the gospel for the salvation of humankind; the shelter, nurture, and spiritual fellowship of the children of God; the maintenance of divine worship; the preservation of truth; the promotion of social righteousness; and the exhibition of the Kingdom of Heaven to the world.
—*Book of Order*, G-1.0200, PC(USA)

The life, death, resurrection, and promised coming of Jesus Christ has set the pattern for the church's mission. His life as man involves the church in the common life of men. His service to men commits the church to work for every form of human well-being. His suffering makes the church sensitive to all the sufferings of mankind so that it sees the face of Christ in the faces of men in every kind of need. His crucifixion discloses to the church God's judgment on man's inhumanity to man and the awful consequences of its own complicity in injustice. In the power of the risen Christ and the hope of his coming, the church sees the promise of God's renewal of man's life in society and of God's victory over all wrong.
—The Confession of 1967, *Book of Confessions* 9.32, PC(USA)

The church follows this pattern in the form of its life and in the method of its action. So to live and serve is to confess Christ as Lord.
—The Confession of 1967, *Book of Confessions* 9.33, PC(USA)

The Christian mission is never self-explanatory, although it is often presented as if it were. Until one understands something of what missionaries wish to bring about through their evangelization, it is impossible to test their authenticity against the authoritative sources of Bible and tradition. Conversion, renewal, and rebirth are certainly biblical concepts but they always provoke other questions: conversion to what, renewal of what, rebirth into what kind of new life? Here as elsewhere the saying of Jesus applies: "By their fruits you shall know them."[1]
—Douglas John Hall

The city is a place of radical extremes. Chicago's average temperature in January is 21 degrees and in July is 73 degrees. But the extremities characterize the place with an annual variable of 115 degrees or so. The temperature was 106 degrees last July—in five months it was sure to drop to minus 10 degrees.

Fourth Presbyterian Church is located in a neighborhood of enormous privilege, affluence, and very conspicuous consumption. Across Michigan Avenue from the church is the John Hancock Center, the fifth tallest building in the nation. Nearly fourteen hundred people live in the 703 Hancock condominium units. The first forty-two stories are occupied by offices, small businesses, and boutiques. On the ground level is a men's clothing store where you can purchase a necktie for a hundred dollars. Diagonally across Michigan Avenue, Lord & Taylor and Marshall Field's anchor Water Tower Place, an enormously successful and popular vertical shopping mall. On Chestnut Street to the south is Escada, an elegant women's apparel shop. To the north, across Delaware Place is the 66-story 900 Building, with another vertical mall anchored by Bloomingdales and Henri Bendel, with the four-star Four Seasons hotel occupying the thirtieth through the forty-sixth floor and nineteen stories of elegant condominiums overlooking the neighborhood. The Westin Hotel, the graceful Drake, the Knickerbocker, the Whitehall, the Tremont, and the Ritz Carlton—all are within one block of Fourth Presbyterian Church.

During every day of the Christmas shopping season, one charter bus after another stops in front of the church at 9:30 A.M. and disgorges determined shoppers from the near and far suburbs and beyond, headed happily to Marshall Field's, Bloomingdales, and all points between for the day. At 6:30 the buses reappear to gather in their thousands of happy, exhausted, and significantly poorer passengers. North Michigan Avenue in Chicago, the Magnificent Mile, has become foot by front foot, the most profitable retail merchandising street in the nation.

The area directly north of the church is known as the Gold Coast, primarily because the city's powerful and privileged elite used to live there. That has changed somewhat. Most of the old mansions are gone, but the area immediately surrounding the church on either side of Michigan Avenue is home to literally thousands of people living in the high- and low-rise apartment buildings, condominiums, and brownstones. Two miles further north, in Lincoln Park, is one of the largest concentrations of young urban professionals in the nation.

One mile directly west of the church is Cabrini-Green, a Chicago Housing Authority complex of high- and low-rise apartments that has come to symbolize everything that is wrong with public housing and urban living. Cabrini-Green, like most of Chicago's public housing, was constructed during the 1950s and 1960s in the midst of a hopeful and exuberantly optimistic effort to eliminate slums and renew our urban areas. It was believed that federal rent subsidies would stimulate economic as well as racial integration. Families would live together in modern, efficient, clean apartments in safe and pleasant neighborhoods. But something went wrong. A lot of things went wrong. Doctoral theses are researched; high-level federal, state, and local conferences are held; a whole library of books by learned urban sociologists, economists, and social scientists has been written attempting to explain what went wrong.

The fact is that one mile from Bloomingdales and the Four Seasons is a community of people living in third-world squalor. Thirteen thousand people live there, mostly women and children, in high-rise apartments where most of the elevators don't work and where those that do are commandeered by gang members and operated for a fee, where the smell of urine in the halls and stairways assaults everyone who walks in, where what used to be a playground is a glass-strewn, blacktop trash dump with no play equipment in sight. Gunfire breaks out regularly at Cabrini. Sometimes from the Hancock Building you can see puffs of white smoke from automatic weapons, like the evening news from Beirut or Sarajevo. Children at Cabrini learn to hit the deck like Marines in combat at the sound of gunfire.

Cabrini is a mystery and an anomaly. Not just Cabrini, but the entire public housing system, and the social/economic/political dynamic that produced it, is much on the minds of people who care about the city, particularly church people.

Cabrini-Green represents the most dramatic contrast to the affluence of the near north side and is therefore God's clearest call to mission for the church. But there are other jarring contrasts as well: homelessness, for instance. It is a delicate and not very savory subject, but our neighborhood is a good place to be if you are destitute because we produce good garbage and lots of it. A homeless person looking desperately for something to eat can find something among the discarded fast food containers in the trash baskets on Michigan Avenue or in the heavily laden dumpsters in the alleys behind four-star restaurants. Our neighborhood is relatively safe. The homeless are terribly vulnerable, frequent victims of assault and rape. Our neighborhood is well lighted, and police are frequently visible. If you are homeless, North Michigan Avenue is not a bad place to spend time.

It is a city of radical contrasts: wealth and poverty, high-end condominiums and homelessness, stability, self-fulfilled well-being and addiction, alienation, desperation, and, of course, the paradox of feeling alone in the middle of the city, the peculiarly intense loneliness that is exacerbated by the happily busy, hurrying masses of humanity all around.

Mission Is Why We Are Here

"The church exists by mission as fire exists by burning," Emil Brunner observed. Mission, our reaching out to our neighbors in the name of Jesus Christ, is the lifeblood of the church. I have come to see this differently, opposite in fact, from the way church people ordinarily think about mission. Typically, we regard mission as the extra work of charity and compassion that we do after we have taken care of all our other responsibilities: to the world—paying the heat and light bills; to the congregation—providing Sunday school classes, pastoral care, and counseling; and to the professionals—paying the minister's salary. When all that is done, mission receives what amounts to our leftover energy, imagination, intelligence, love, and resources.

I have thought like this. I have come to be convinced that thinking like this, understandable and logical as it is, is in fact part of what is wrong with us. We are not called simply to exist. We are not called just to survive. We are not even called to be successful. We are called, as churches, to be faithful to Jesus Christ and to serve the world as he served it, to love the world as he loved it, to give our lives away to the world as he gave his life away. The resources to live, to exist, and to survive are given to us by God, not so much as we become more efficient, more economical, more astute at raising funds and conserving our resources (as important as that is), but precisely as we discover that the reason for the church's being is simply mission.

Jean Bethke Elshtain has written an important new book, *Democracy on Trial*, which proposes that the hope for a meaningful future will result from a renewal of citizenship, public-spirited concern for the public, the community. Professor Elshtain in a recent lecture spoke of the importance of the churches for the life of their cities, communities, and neighborhoods. The simple existence of a church enhances the quality of life in a neighborhood, she said. Strangely, even crime statistics are better in the neighborhoods around churches.

Churches serve the city in at least three ways:

First, churches serve by their presence, by being there, by reminding the whole community of mutuality and the basic human responsibility to care for and about one another.

Second, churches serve by providing community, by providing space, opportunity, and reason for otherwise busy and preoccupied people to be together. Churches are reminders that life can be lived a little more gently, kindly, peaceably.

And third, churches serve the city, in one of our oldest traditions, by serving the needs, by opening doors to, and reaching out to those who are most fragile, most vulnerable.

Thomas Jefferson is said to have proposed that democracies require a revolution every generation or so to clear away the clutter and remind the people of what the basic purpose of the enterprise is. Implicit in his suggestion is something that we have learned experientially, namely, that organizations and the bureaucracies that work in them, are inclined to drift away, over time, from their basic, foundational purposes. If left to their own devices, organizations will, in time, devote their energy and resources to their own survival and not to whatever purpose called them into existence in the first place. At regular intervals the U.S. Post Office must find a way to remind itself and all its employees that its purpose is to deliver the mail; the school system, to teach children; and General Motors, to manufacture automobiles that people want to purchase. And likewise the church—at regular intervals we need to remind ourselves of our purpose for being, that we exist to do the work of Jesus Christ in the world—the mission. And at regular intervals we need to define what the particulars of our mission are.

This process, sometimes called long-range planning or strategic planning, is absolutely critical if we are to remain faithful to our Lord. In the Presbyterian Church (U.S.A.), this basic planning and evaluating, leading to a renewal of the congregation's sense of mission, is built into the life of the institution by way of a requirement for each congregation to do a self-study and write a mission statement at the time a pastor resigns and before a new search committee goes to work. Presbyterians complain about it a lot. It seems like nothing more than bureaucratic busy work created by an office in denominational headquarters light years away from the actual life of an actual congregation.

But corporate grumbling aside, every congregation needs regularly to look at itself and the needs of its neighbors and to redefine its mission.

At Fourth Presbyterian Church the process was undertaken in a major way when my predecessor, Dr. Elam Davies, retired after a distinguished twenty-three-year ministry. Under Elam's careful guidance a representative group of church members looked at the church and its programs, looked with equal commitment at the city and the church's neighbors, and wrote a mission statement, a strategic plan. The essence of it was that Fourth Church needed to broaden and deepen its mission outreach programs, its opportunities for worship, education, and mission involvement.

During the prior twenty years the church had initiated a number of outreach ministries mission projects. For example, the Lorene Replogle Counseling Center, housed in an adjacent church-owned building, offers a full range of therapeutic services provided by its director and a staff of professional therapists. The cost of the service is determined for each client on the basis of ability to pay. The clients of the counseling center come from the congregation and from the community at large. In addition to personal counseling, during the year the center offers group therapy and a variety of workshops on personal, emotional, relational, and spiritual topics. Couples who are married at Fourth Presbyterian Church participate in a two-hour premarital consultation with one of the center's therapists.

The Center for Older Adults, located within the church complex, is a ministry of connection, relationship, life-enhancement, health services, activity, and spiritual growth.

The Elam Davies Social Service Center, "The Door," offers basic services, food, clothing, personal consultation, and referrals to walk-in clients and visitors daily. This center occupies an apartment complex on the church's ground level.

The tutoring program brings together city youngsters, mostly from Cabrini-Green, with volunteer tutors once a week for two-hour sessions of remedial academic work.

The church's commitment to broaden and deepen its mission in the city, identified and articulated in the 1985 Strategic Plan, was the mandate for a new ministry when I arrived as pastor. With the support of the officers we went to work to fulfill the mandate.

For example, we asked the counseling center to continue its good work, to see more clients, and to communicate its presence and services to the community.

We made major commitments to expand the scope of our mission through the Center for Older Adults and the tutoring program by hiring full-time directors for each and setting both programs to work on an accelerated basis. The results have been dramatic. More older adults are relating to the Center, participating in its activities. A part-time health professional, a parish nurse, was retained. And the Center for Older Adults now offers basic health consultations and referrals, and Fourth Church has a new and critical dimension in the pastoral care available to our members and friends. Our nurse formerly worked in geriatrics at Rush Presbyterian St. Luke's and Northwestern hospitals. She knows her field, is a committed Christian, and among other activities, arranges an annual health fair for our neighbors and a free immunization program in cooperation with the city of Chicago's Department of Public Health and our partner hospitals, which last year provided free inoculation to 3,410 people.

The new Director of Educational Outreach and Tutoring brought together the parts of the existing programs and with our new Associate Pastor for Mission, who has a vision for urban ministry, went to work expanding our horizons and our sense of mission. The director is a veteran Chicago Public School teacher, an educator, a Christian, and a true entrepreneur. In short order the number of youngsters enrolled in tutoring increased from 200 to 500. So did the number of volunteer tutors recruited, trained, and organized. The Tutoring Director and the Associate Pastor for Mission established a not-for-profit corporation, Partners in Education (PIE), to coordinate our community education and activities and to receive corporate and foundation grants not ordinarily available to churches. In addition to tutoring, PIE includes a scholarship program for several youngsters per year at a small group of private schools and colleges, a summer day program for 125 city youngsters, and a values education program at the public school that serves Cabrini-Green. The PIE budget has doubled since 1990 to $134,000; 43 percent of their budget comes from the Fourth Presbyterian Mission budget.

The Tutoring Director and her advisory committee have persuaded local businesses to donate computers to the program so our youngsters can spend a half hour per night working on one of the twelve units in our computer center. Volunteers offer piano lessons, ballet, and personal grooming consultations, and a growing group of tutoring parents meet together with church members for fellowship and discussion.

We have had to learn to be responsive to the realities of the city. Four years ago the numbers of youngsters attending tutoring from Cabrini-Green dropped suddenly and dramatically. We talked about it among ourselves and tried to identify the reason. Perhaps we weren't doing something right. Maybe the kids were bored and losing interest. Maybe it was the attraction of television. Finally, having exhausted all the alternatives, we asked some mothers who we knew historically had made certain their children were in our programs but who had been conspicuously absent recently.

They told us a hard and stunning truth. The gang activity in the city that has increased so dramatically and dangerously around the crack-cocaine epidemic and the easy accessibility of firearms were the reasons their youngsters weren't coming to Fourth Presbyterian Church's tutoring program. There were, the mothers patiently explained, two clear gang boundaries between Cabrini-Green and Fourth Presbyterian Church. No parents who cared about their children were going to allow them to walk to Fourth Presbyterian and across those boundaries, particularly after dark. We had always wondered whether the tutoring program ought to be held in or at least close to Cabrini instead of in our big, intimidating gothic church on the Magnificent Mile. We thought the program might seem patronizing and elitist, importing predominantly poor African-American children to our predominantly white, comfortable church for an evening and then sending them home. "Forget it," our Cabrini mothers told us. "We want our children to be there, to see the church and Michigan Avenue." I'll never forget one of the mothers telling me that until her son attended the tutoring program, he had never before even seen Michigan Avenue. We had always known it was good for Fourth Presbyterian Church to be the home of the tutoring program; then we knew that the children and their parents wanted to be there, too. So we initiated a busing program. Every week night a big yellow school bus picks up youngsters in Cabrini, deposits them at church, and then takes them home again at the end of the evening. We provided the buses and adult monitors for supervisors, and the children returned to tutoring in greater numbers than ever.

This busing program creates a human tableau that makes me smile every time I see it. The entry door that the youngsters use for tutoring, where the bus stops to drop them off, is directly across the street from the Four Seasons hotel. It's not a wide street. A parked school bus full of happy, noisy youngsters does not go unnoticed and, in fact, creates a major disruption. Taxis are arriving from O'Hare with Four Seasons guests. Other taxis are lined up waiting for departing fares. There are always plenty of people coming and going, most of them elegantly attired for an evening out in the city. The doorman and bell boys are hustling to and fro. And across the street, fifty feet away, youngsters pour out of a bus to meet their tutors and spend an evening together. It makes me smile, and it always reminds me of something Jesus said about welcoming the little ones, allowing the children to come to him.

As the program grows, funding becomes critical and difficult. So we hustle. The director corresponds with supporters all over the Midwest and asks for money. Tutoring kids participate in a Christmas art contest. The five winning pictures are used on Christmas cards, printed on donated stock, and sold at the church, and increasingly, at local bookstores. Three thousand seven hundred fifty boxes of cards were sold last year, and more will be printed and sold this year. Most significant of all, we finally have corporate support. Quaker Oats, whose corporate headquarters is a few blocks away, has a good community program called Kid's Cafe. That company supplies food and money to administer the program, and we offer our tutoring program kids a hot meal before they go to work with their tutors and a nutritious breakfast in the summer.

New programs were initiated to enable the church to respond to the heartbreaking increase of homeless people on the streets of Chicago. Exact numbers are difficult to establish, and experts from different political and ideological perspectives differ radically in their estimates of the number of homeless men, women, and children on the Chicago streets. What we know is that there are a lot; many more now than there used to be.

Our efforts began with a task force to plan our response, and out of it came a Fourth Church-sponsored shelter on the near west side, a Sunday night supper in the church dining room for anyone who wants and needs to eat, and a cooking for the homeless program that enlists volunteers to plan, purchase, prepare, and deliver hot meals to a number of north side shelters. A Habitat for Humanity component constructed houses and remodeled apartments, and a new program, "Cabrini-Alive," takes volunteer workers and supplies into Cabrini-Green every Saturday morning to clean and fix up individual apartments with the full participation of the residents.

After ten years we stepped back, looked at ourselves, and asked again about the needs of our neighbors and what more God might be calling us to do and to be. Two important initiatives have resulted.

The Center for Whole Life at Cabrini-Green is a Fourth Church presence, finally, inside the project. We rent an apartment, and a small staff, augmented by volunteers, talks with residents, provides a clean, safe place for a cup of coffee, willing listeners, and toys for the children. Classes in nutrition, child care, and employment are offered, and each week there is a prayer meeting that remarkably brings together a group of adults from Cabrini and Fourth Presbyterian Church—separated by an enormous social and economic gap, but united in common humanity and faith in Jesus Christ.

The recently opened Fourth Church Children's Center, our newest project, is a full day-care center for the neighborhood, created in our building as part of our major renovation and rebuilding project. The Fourth Church Children's Center will provide safe and healthy child care for sixty-three families, 20 percent of whom will receive scholarship assistance.

Fourth Presbyterian Church is an unusual congregation in an unusual situation. The church has resources that make it unique; and we do not tell the story of our mission in order to boast or to cause other congregations in very different situations to feel inadequate. Rather, we believe we have rediscovered an old and critical truth about the church—that we exist for mission and that when we allow the gospel of Jesus Christ to define and direct the church, we find ourselves inevitably living our institutional life, not merely to service, but for the sake of the world God so loves.

The Church Exists for the World

I have learned two things from our experience that are of general use. First, mission, however ambitious and expensive or modest and inexpensive, is not an optional activity for the church. It is not the work we do after we have taken care of our responsibility to ourselves and paid all our other bills. It is the reason we exist. Of course, the churches are communities of support and pastoral care for their members, and of course, churches educate and nurture and worship. But if the church is not engaged in some mission, some outreach to the community, to the world, a vital dimension of the church both as institution and as the gospel, the evangel, which the church represents, is missing.

Second, mission requires leadership, commitment, and a process that allows a local church to identify the needs of its neighbors, the church's capacity—realized or unrealized—to meet those needs, and a place to do it; in short, strategic planning.

Before we launched our renovation project and set out to raise the funds to support it, we rolled up our sleeves and did it again: another strategic plan. We asked our officers and leaders to identify and express their hopes and dreams for their church. We prayed about it a lot. And we asked our neighbors, our community, the city, what they needed and wanted from the church. It's hard work. It requires an investment of time and energy that we sometimes feel would be better used in the work itself. But taking the time and marshaling the resources and organizing the process to ask the community about its needs is absolutely essential. Knowing the question, after all, is a prerequisite to an appropriate answer. Taking time to listen is a way of caring about and loving others.

Part of the process for this strategic plan was writing a mission statement. The process itself is very helpful and can be adopted for any congregation's use. We were fortunate enough to have among our church leadership people who earn their livings as planners and who help organizations—businesses, mainly, but also schools and hospitals and museums—to identify their basic purposes and to write their mission statements. Allan Cox met with the church staff at a 24-hour retreat and in several shorter follow-up meetings, conducted a workshop for all church officers and all committee members, and worked with a writing team to produce the final document.

Allan's only rule—which was never, under any circumstances to be broken—was 75 words. "If you can't say it in 75 words, you don't know what it is, and besides, nobody will read it," he told us again and again. At first I thought he was oversimplifying this complex institution. And then I received a copy of the mission statement of a theological seminary that includes me on its mailing list. The mission statement was four pages and single-spaced. The accompanying document explaining what the mission statement meant was twenty pages. I scanned the papers quickly and learned that the seminary intended essentially to reorganize all of Western civilization and to re-create the Holy Catholic Church. I returned to Allan's rule with new attentiveness.

We did it. It was not easy, but it was not unpleasant. In fact, we had fun, and before it was over, the church leadership felt a sense of ownership and then pride: pride in Fourth Presbyterian Church and

humble gratitude for the privilege of being the church of Jesus
Christ, of being agents and ambassadors of God's love in Jesus
Christ.

This is the mission statement we produced:

> We are a light in the city
> reflecting the inclusive love of God.
>
> Comforted and challenged by the Gospel of Christ,
> we strive to be a welcoming, serving community.
>
> At the intersection of faith and life, we share God's grace
> through worship, preaching, education and ministries of
> healing, reconciliation and justice.
>
> We affirm the worth of all and nurture each individual's
> spiritual pilgrimage.
> Inspired by our heritage, we confront our future with hope
> and confidence in God's purpose.

We use our mission statement a lot. Because we adhered to
Allan's "75-word" rule, albeit reluctantly, our mission statement is
usable. It fits in a side column in our newsletter. We can even use it
liturgically. We know that it was not handed down to us from heav-
en and that it has limits. We know that we must revise it in a few
years for the very reason that the world around us continues to
change and so will the needs of our community.

Martin Marty says that "the seven last words of the church" will
be, "We never did it that way before." It is not easy for an institution with a two-thousand-year-old history to change, to think new
thoughts, and to engage in new behavior. But faithfulness to our
Lord and to our own reason for being—the mission of representing
and living God's love for a changing world—demands it.

I served a church in Scotland one summer. It was one of the best
things we ever did as a family. It was also good experience in the
practice of ministry and the leading of a church. We have dear
friends in that Scottish village still, and I have a deep respect and
abiding affection for the Church of Scotland, the ecclesiastical parent of American Presbyterianism. Both American and Scottish
Presbyterians are in numerical decline and in what feels sometimes
like a spiritual depression. In Scotland, the church is part of the fab-
ric of the culture, far more so than in the United States. In every village the kirk is part of the establishment, along with the bank, police
station, and town hall. But fewer and fewer Scots attend church

these days. It feels as if the Church of Scotland, like the English and their state church, is becoming a marginal religious ornament in Scottish culture.

In our village the church was the largest and by far the grandest structure, built one hundred years ago to accommodate every person in the entire parish. The sanctuary seated fifteen hundred, but only one hundred souls regularly showed up for worship on a good Sunday. During the week the beautiful church was kept tightly locked.

Directly across the street from the church and the manse where we were living was one of Scotland's busiest and most profitable woolen mills, a routine stop for all the tour buses traveling up and down Scotland's west coast. Every day I would watch from my study window as the tourists left their bus, entered the mill to purchase sweaters and scarves, emerged from the mill, and on the way back to the bus noticed the high spire and graceful facade of the church. Inevitably, they crossed the road, walked to the entrance, tried the door—unsuccessfully, of course—walked around the building trying each door, and finally, prevented from entering, walked away from the church and returned to the bus.

My Scottish parishioners did not expect me to do more than preach and visit the members, but I could not resist asking a question and making a suggestion. "Why don't we open the church doors?" I asked. "We could recruit a few volunteers to be present to greet and show the visitors around a bit, maybe even have some literature available about the building, the Church of Scotland?"

My friends looked at me quizzically. "Why would we want to do that?" they asked me.

I was delighted to learn recently that they are doing it now. Their beloved kirk is open, and people are seeing it and, maybe, thinking about the mysterious presence of the holy in life that the church building represents and about the Lord the church proclaims and whose body every church is called to be.

An important part of being the church of Jesus Christ is to know the world, to be a part of the world. And the way to do that is to observe our communities carefully and to ask our neighbors to tell us about their needs, hopes, fears, aspirations.

Being a church in the middle of the human community means joining the search for authentic spirituality, the quest for meaning, the hunger for truth. Being the church means being in the world, thoroughly and unapologetically. And it means serving; giving something of life away in order to live fully and authentically. There is something about the mission—the intentional outreach, the consistent asking after the needs of the community, the neighborhood, the world—that authenticates and celebrates and communicates the message of the gospel.

The marginalization of religion that the sociologists are observing in American life happens in individual lives. Faith is squeezed into a corner, closeted from the rest of life, kept pure, untainted by politics, economics. The Athenians did that intellectually; they played with the ideas of faith and religion but could not deal with the particularities of the God Paul proclaimed, the One who raised Jesus from the dead.

The Athenians were on the right track in their pursuit of truth; they were asking the right questions with their altar to an unknown God. But they couldn't get their minds around the incarnation, the actual involvement of God in the daily life of creation and human history. Their god was an abstraction, their religion devoid of passion.

I've always loved that wonderful image Søren Kierkegaard invoked and taught. He called it the "leap of faith." Reason and intellectual inquiry can take us only so far. Having thought about and analyzed and discussed religion, we can either pull away, marginalize the whole business, keep it safely separate from the rest of life, or with everything in us—heart and soul and mind and strength—make a decision to believe, to trust, to commit. It is, as Kierkegaard called it, a leap into an abyss, a leap of faith, a loving entrusting of ourselves to God.

There is something of that in being a church, in a building whose architectural style was popular several centuries ago, growing smaller in relation to the institutions around us by the decade yet bravely proclaiming the presence of One who is sovereign over all, in this place where human achievement is displayed in stark contrast with human failure and despair. It is precisely here, speaking a word of kindness and hope, praying and working for a future of justice and peace, extending a hand of welcome and compassion to the neediest: the city of God, here on a corner in the city of Chicago.

There is always something of that in being a Christian, here or anywhere. It is always a leap of faith to believe in God, to trust God, to follow Jesus. It is always a leap of faith to commit all of life, even our death, to God, the One who calls us individually as God's people and corporately as God's church, to live fully and faithfully and responsibly. It is always a leap of trust in the One in whom we do "live and move and have our being."

O God, you are my God, I seek you,
    my soul thirsts for you;
my flesh faints for you,
    as in a dry and weary land
        where there is no water.
So I have looked upon you in
    the sanctuary, . . .
your steadfast love is
    better than life,
    my lips will praise you.
So I will bless you as long as I live . . .
                    (Psalm 63:1–4)

3

The People

The true church is the whole community, on earth and in heaven, of those called by God into fellowship with him and with one another to know and do his will. As the body of Christ, the Church on earth is the instrument through which God continues to proclaim and apply the benefits of his redemptive work and to establish his Kingdom.
—*A Brief Statement of Belief*,
Presbyterian Church in the United States, 1962

God the Holy Spirit fulfills the work of reconciliation in man. The Holy Spirit creates and renews the church as the community in which men are reconciled to God and to one another.
—The Confession of 1967, *Book of Confessions* 9.20, PC(USA)

God's redeeming work in Jesus Christ embraces the whole of man's life: social and cultural, economic and political, scientific and technological, individual and corporate.
—The Confession of 1967, *Book of Confessions* 9.53, PC(USA)

Members of this generation are asking questions about the meaning of their lives, about what they want for themselves and for their children. They are still exploring, as they did in their years growing up, but now they are exploring in new and, we think, more profound ways. Religion and spiritual themes are surfacing in a rich variety of ways—in Eastern religion, in evangelical and fundamentalist teaching, in mysticism and new age movements, in Goddess worship and other ancient religious rituals, in the mainline churches and synagogues, in Twelve-Step recovery groups, in concern about the environment, in holistic health, in personal and social transformation. Many within this generation who dropped out of churches and synagogues years ago are now shopping around for a congregation.[1]
—Wade Clark Roof

Two major developments have changed the situation for the churches in our culture. The first is that mainline churches continue to decline in numbers, influence, and power. Second, Americans, particularly the much-studied population cohort called Baby Boomers, are on a religious quest, seeking, searching, asking religious questions as never before.

Some are church shopping. Some are turning to the new megachurches. And some are returning to the traditional churches. Many of them are watching, listening, waiting.

Who comes to church, and why? And how can we respond faithfully to the major forces in the culture out of our lively tradition?

One of the dimensions of contemporary life about which working clergypersons know almost nothing is what people do on Sunday morning, what life is like on Sunday morning. We've read Wallace Stevens about the increasingly redundant "holy hush" of a sabbath morning, and we occasionally complain when someone invades what we have come to think is our privileged territory—the time between 9:00 A.M. and noon on the first day of the week, the Chicago Marathon, for instance, which uses Michigan Avenue and Lake Shore Drive, and makes driving downtown a very tentative project. When the Chicago Bears kick off in Soldier Field at noon, which they always do to accommodate the tight Sunday television schedule, many of our 11:00 worshipers come at 8:30, some choose our 6:30 Vesper Service, many don't worship at all, and few of those who do stay afterward for coffee and conversation.

One Sunday morning, like a tourist in a foreign land, I found myself at home in Chicago with nothing to do. I was not supposed to be there, but our Michigan vacation was interrupted by some family business and I decided to stay over in Chicago on Sunday morning, sneak into the south balcony, see what worship was like, and hear one of my colleagues preach.

Faced with a wonderfully empty three hours on a Sunday morning, I decided to go for a bike ride on the lake front. It was glorious. It was also an experience that I have been thinking about ever since, so much so, in fact, that I now believe all working clergypersons and seminary students should intentionally experience what people who do not attend worship do on Sunday morning.

The lake front on a clear, pleasant, summer Sunday morning is a wonder to behold. The sun rising over Lake Michigan glistens off bright water. The lake front walkway, which thanks to visionary urban planners of Chicago like Daniel Burnham, extends uninterrupted all the way to the far south side and north to Evanston, a total of eighteen miles, was full of people—people walking seriously with

Sony Walkmans plugged in their ears, people strolling or walking dogs, joggers of all ages, sizes, and shapes, rollerbladers, skateboarders, and bicyclists on the full range of racers, mountain, trail, and cruiser bikes available. I fell into the flow, marveling at all this pleasant activity. At North Avenue Beach, volleyball games were already in progress, and preparation for a professional tournament, sponsored by a major beer company, to start at 11:00 was under way in a frenzy of activity. Further up the lake front, families had already spread blankets, and some were cooking breakfast sausage on portable charcoal grills. Boaters were assembling gear, setting sails, and heading out through Belmont and Montrose harbors. When I arrived at the public golf course at Recreation Drive, where urban duffers were already well into eighteen holes, I made my second important decision to do something I had never done before. I stopped at the small cafe that sits between the golf course and the bike path and ordered one of their legendary omelettes, toast, juice, and coffee. The outdoor tables were full of happy people, talking, eating, reading. I found a discarded *New York Times* and read it while waiting for my omelette. And then, the defining moment: This is wonderful! I thought. What luxury! What a beautiful city! What a great way to spend a Sunday morning! Why would anybody want to do anything else with the exquisite gift of a free and pleasant morning in Chicago than be on the lake front, drinking coffee, reading the newspaper, waiting for a delicious Denver omelette?

Sunday morning, which the church claims as its private preserve, functions as a blissful enclave in time for people who do not attend church, and it is, I discovered, an attractive alternative to public worship. In the city, or in towns and villages anywhere, in lives that are increasingly busy and a work week that now approaches sixty or seventy hours for many professionals and workers, the investment of several free hours on a Sunday morning to attend church is a big deal. It is, in fact, from the perspective of the lake front cafe table, a countercultural act.

The city is a wonderful place on Sunday morning. There are many interesting and pleasant things to do. If we expect people to give that time to the church, we had better know about and understand the alternatives available and, I think, develop a grateful respect that significant numbers of people get out of bed, dress up, make the trek to church, and give us the morning. Many of them, in spite of our patient explanations of the dangers of pantheism, finding God exclusively in nature, persist in believing that God is just as accessible to them—if not more so—on the golf course and lake front as in church. So the simple fact is people give valuable time to us, the church; it is time they could be using to exercise some of the enticing and attractive recreational and leisure-time alternatives the culture offers.

Meanwhile, at the corner of Michigan Avenue and Delaware Place and at thousands of other places of worship across the land, that countercultural activity is taking place. It is not exactly a demonstration; although, all things considered, it is something of that. Since 8:00 A.M., a steady stream of people has been converging on the gray gothic building on the corner, entering its doors, greeting one another on its sidewalks, drinking coffee, and talking with one another in its courtyard. At 10:30, the activity increases in intensity. Now there are a lot of people converging on the site, exiting taxis and buses, walking from all directions, cars stopping to let children out and heading for one of the nearby parking lots—hundreds of people now pouring through the huge doors over which is this carved inscription: "The Master Is Here and Calleth for Thee." What in the world is going on here?

This countercultural activity that is so very different from the pleasant alternatives available is "church." Hans Kung observes that church is an "event" that happens "when people meet together, pray together, celebrate together—wherever, however, and whenever—as disciples of Christ and in memory of him."[2]

Some of the people who arrive at the door of the gray gothic building know one another and exchange greetings, nods, smiles, handshakes, an occasional hug. Their arrival is a reunion, a homecoming. Many, however, seem to know no one. Arriving alone or in pairs, they seem tentative, not sure what to expect.

Inside the massive wooden doors, ushers and greeters welcome each person and in gestures at once comfortable but obviously intentional and practiced, guide each through the crowded narthex into the large sanctuary, where a series of ushers, men and women identified by dark suits, guide each to a pew, carefully filling the sanctuary from front to back. The ushers recognize many of the worshipers and seat them in places they are accustomed to sitting. A pipe organ is playing strong German baroque music from the eighteenth century. By 11:00 o'clock, every one of the fourteen hundred pew seats is occupied, and many people are gathering in the narthex. Three clergy, two men and a woman, enter the chancel at the front of the sanctuary dressed in black robes with two white strips of cloth, Geneva tabs, attached to white clerical collars. The choir emerges in the loft, facing the gathered congregation. The organ begins a gradual modulation at the end of the Bach and arrives at a refrain so familiar the congregation immediately recognizes it and, as one, rises and sings:

> Praise God from whom all blessings flow
> Praise God all creatures here below
> Praise God above ye heavenly Host
> Praise Father, Son and Holy Ghost.

Why are all these people doing this? A startling number of academicians and researchers who study human behavior say they shouldn't be and, in fact, in significantly increasing numbers, are not attending church on Sunday morning.

Wade Clark Roof and William McKinney, in *American Mainline Religion*, document the changes that have occurred in the traditional religious attitudes of American people, the privileged Protestant mainline's fall from influence and power, the rise of secular humanism as a force hostile to traditional morality. Dean Hoge, Benton Johnson, and Donald Luidens, in their study of Baby Boomers' religion, *Vanishing Boundaries*, observe that the central fact of religious life in our time is the decline of mainline Protestantism and that the postwar generation—the Baby Boomers, particularly—have dropped out of the church. Roof, in his most recent book, *A Generation of Seekers*, argues that Baby Boomers, those Americans born between 1946 and 1964, are influenced more by inner feelings and their own personal choices than by older notions of religious authority. The result is religious individualism. Baby Boomers are seekers, not joiners, but Roof observes that "boomers will commit themselves to religious activities and organizations, including traditional congregations, where they feel there is some authentic connection with their lives and experiences."[3]

Why Are They Here and Not in a Megachurch?

The sanctuary at Fourth Presbyterian Church on Sunday morning is full of the kind of people the experts say should not be there. There are many young adults—Baby Boomers, some middle-aged and elderly—but the gathered congregation on Sunday morning is remarkable because it is predominantly young.

It is intriguing and of more than passing interest to those of us who care about the mainline churches that concurrently with our apparent decline, a new kind of religious institution has emerged—the megachurch. Huge, conspicuously successful, numerically and financially strong, congregations may be found throughout the country.

Fourth Presbyterian Church is not a megachurch. We qualify on the basis of the number of people who attend worship on Sunday, the criteria some analysts use to define a megachurch—two thousand or more. But we don't do any of the distinctive things that megachurches do. We are conspicuously traditional; mainline Presbyterian traditional. Our clergy wear black robes, clerical collars, and Geneva tabs. We sing hymns from *The Hymnal*, most of them classics like, "Holy, Holy, Holy," "When Morning Gilds the Skies," "Joyful, Joyful, We Adore Thee." Our choir is a classical ensemble that presents elegant sacred music Sunday after Sunday, specializing in English, German, and Italian baroque. One local newspaper writer, Bill Grainger, cracked that "if you want to hear Latin on Sunday morning, don't bother with Holy Name Cathedral: go to hear the Fourth Presbyterian Church Morning Choir!" The preacher stands in a pulpit and talks for twenty, sometimes twenty-five minutes. It is traditional, mainline Presbyterian worship.

It is easy for those of us who are struggling to minister faithfully and effectively in traditional mainline churches to be critical of the new megachurches—too easy, in fact. Some of the criticism is simple institutional envy. They are growing, and we are not. In terms of the criteria of success, our culture's favorite criteria, they look more successful than many of us do. Their numbers are better. In the mainline churches there is a remnant, to be sure, of the tired 1960s suspicion of any organization that succeeds by the criteria of American culture. There is at least a remnant of the suspicion that numerical growth is inevitably a signal that a church is doing something wrong, selling out, playing the religion market, maybe even worshiping at the altar of the neo-baalism of American consumer culture. Before we engage in that kind of breast-beating, however, perhaps we ought to inquire, simply and honestly, whether the megachurches know something we have forgotten and whether they may be faithful in ways we have overlooked.

There's a lot about the whole megachurch phenomena that contradicts my own liturgical and aesthetic mainline Presbyterianism. And I have serious questions about the intentional amnesia of some megachurches when it comes to church history. Their determined efforts to not look, feel, or sound like traditional churches leave me with the distinct impression that some enthusiastic adherents think the gospel of Jesus Christ and the Holy Catholic Church were invented in this decade.

But a number of megachurches work. I believe the megachurches succeed in an area of ministry in which the more traditional, mainline churches continue to fail, namely, in proclaiming the gospel to and attracting people who long ago dismissed church and faith and stopped taking religion seriously. Wade Clark Roof says they are seeking, looking for something important enough to claim their devotion, even shopping for a congregation. Many of them are going to megachurches.

Outside Chicago in the western suburb of Barrington, Willow Creek Community Church is a vital and growing megachurch that attracts literally thousands of young adults. Recent media documentaries have featured Willow Creek, including an ABC special and a four-part, front-page series in the *New York Times*.

Good things happen at Willow Creek. Individual lives are transformed, families are strengthened, relationships are supported. Good things happen in the community because of Willow Creek's outside enterprises.

In fact, I think that the megachurches may be serving, albeit unconsciously, an evangelistic and life-giving purpose for the mainline churches. It would not be the first time that God chose to do a new thing to enliven and energize the people of God for the future. I think that megachurch members will increasingly find their way back into mainline churches. When the people of Willow Creek's highly mobile suburban congregation move to new communities, my prediction is that substantial numbers of them will be joining Methodist, Presbyterian, and Lutheran congregations.

What I hope will not happen in the meantime is that struggling mainline congregations will attempt to imitate the booming megachurches. Could it be that in our sincere but desperate efforts to reverse the numerical decline, we have too quickly and too simply attributed the decline to our traditions and dropped them like ecclesiastical hot potatoes, exchanged our pews for theater seats, transformed our sermons into chatty monologues, dismissed the great music of the faith in favor of more upbeat praise music? I think we make a mistake when we try to imitate the megachurches. I believe the tradition itself has a built-in liveliness that we have overlooked. I believe that our Presbyterian, Methodist, Lutheran, and Roman Catholic traditions still speak as profoundly to basic human needs as they ever did and thus communicate the truth, hope, and promise of the gospel of Jesus Christ. What is called for is a recovery of our tradition, a reexamination that will result in our reclaiming and honoring, employing and celebrating our traditions as energetically and imaginatively as we are able.

There is a liveliness about the Reformed tradition that calls the church to self-examination, renewal, and creativity. Presbyterian theologian Brian Gerrish says that the motto of the Reformation, "reformed and always willing to be reformed according to the word of God and the call of the Spirit," is a "habit of the mind" for us. Our tradition was born in a time of intellectual upheaval. John Calvin knew about Copernicus and lived and worked in a world that was learning how to think anew. Calvin, according to Gerrish, borrowed heavily from the Renaissance humanists to create a "Christian philosophy" that was at once grounded in scripture and tradition but also conversant with the new developments in the world around it.[4]

The genius of Calvinism, as it has been expressed in the Reformed tradition, is the principle of criticism: self-criticism. The best of our tradition, that is to say, is its commitment to a process that subjects the church to constant critical inquiry and produces regularly a lively and creative response. It is, by nature, a very lively tradition.

Looking for a Lively Tradition

Who are they, these extraordinary people who not only are engaging in countercultural activity on Sunday morning but are also joining the church, investing significant amounts of their time in the church, serving their neighbors through the church, giving money to the church, finding in the church a focused center for their lives?

There is a great moment when participants in the new members class at Fourth Church introduce themselves to members of the Session. We receive new members during worship once a month. Our Inquirers Class is offered twice monthly, taught by a staff/laity team, and is required for membership. Between twenty-five and thirty-five people join the church every month. On the Sunday morning of their reception they meet first with the Session, and they sit together in worship for the formal ceremonial reception, welcome, and baptism as appropriate.

At the beginning of the Session meeting, which precedes their formal, public reception to membership and which is the way persons become members of a Presbyterian congregation, they stand up one at a time to introduce themselves, to tell a bit about their personal religious journey, and to share whatever they are comfortable sharing of their reasons for deciding to affirm or reaffirm their personal faith in Jesus Christ and commit themselves to the life, ministry, and mission of Fourth Presbyterian Church. It is, of course, testimony time, although we would not think of using that word to say what it is.

It is a great moment, and it regularly moves me and all the ministers and elders in the room deeply. Some of the people are new to the neighborhood and are transferring their membership from churches in other communities. Some of them are suburbanites who drive into the city for church because they care about the life of the city and want to be a part of what Fourth Church means to the city. One of the more interesting emerging phenomenon at Fourth Church is long-distance, commuter membership. One couple, a physician and a nurse, drive in from Valparaiso, Indiana—a distance of sixty miles. Both are active members, serving on boards and committees. They are emptynesters, and they make a day of it every Sunday, attending adult Sunday school and worship at Fourth Church, enjoying lunch and an afternoon in the city—a concert, a movie, the theater, a musical—then attend 6:30 Vespers before heading home to Indiana. Many others drive downtown, an easy commute on Sunday from close-in or distant suburbs: Oak Park, River Forest, Evanston, Lake Forest. Regular Fourth Church members commute from Hinsdale, twenty miles, Schaumburg, thirty-two miles, and Naperville, thirty-eight miles, and they never miss a meeting.

In his classic study, *The Suburban Captivity of the Church* (Doubleday & Co., 1961), Gibson Winter proposed a new configuration for a "larger parish" that avoided the social and economic stratification of American churches by cutting across and through the neighborhood boundaries, or concentric rings that characterize a modern city by cutting through the social and economic stratification and the American urban areas. Parishes, Winter hoped, would be pie-slice-shaped, from the furthest suburbs extending to the very heart of the city, drawing from, serving, and unifying all the economic, racial, and social strata it intersected. Something like this actually happens at Fourth Church.

Our most unusual commuters live in Bowling Green, Ohio, three hundred fifty miles away. Both of them are academic researchers, and their business brings them to Chicago six or seven times a year. They became acquainted with Fourth Church on one of their professional trips and found themselves attracted to our workshops, music, and outreach programs. They made an appointment and told me they had thought and prayed about it and wanted to join our church. I tried unsuccessfully to encourage them to join a church in their community and to continue their regular visitor, mailing list, and contributor relationship with us. They explained patiently that they traveled so much that they were rarely at home on weekends, and besides, they thought it was a better idea to relate to a congregation on the basis of theological and missional affinity than on simple geography. "But 350 miles!" I protested.

"We'll be there more frequently than some of the members on your roll," Milt quipped. And he has been right, of course.

A new long-distance, commuter membership emerges in each new-member class. Others join because they are planning to be married, and they want to begin their new life in church.

Only one in five of our three hundred new members each year is a Presbyterian by background, so part of our new member orientation is familiarizing inquirers with a little of our history, tradition, and vocabulary, and inevitably explaining that predestination is not the same as philosophic fatalism and that when the cat died suddenly and mysteriously, it was not in God's plan.

The personal stories that move me most come from what is actually the largest group of our new members and the people who increasingly dominate the congregation—young urban professionals between the ages of 25 and 40, most of them single, most of them successfully engaged in their professional careers, most of them newcomers to church or returning to what they like to call "organized religion" (If only they knew how unorganized Fourth Church is sometimes!) after an absence of ten to twenty years. They are surgical residents at Northwestern Memorial Hospital, attorneys, traders at the Mercantile Exchange, advertising executives. Some are between jobs, some are starting new jobs, some are changing careers. Some are actors, actresses, salespersons, market researchers, and graduate students, and what they say when they introduce themselves to the Session, sometimes haltingly, sometimes with fluent simplicity, sometimes tearfully, always eloquently, is something like this:

> I'm working hard. I'm very busy. My life is consumed by my job. For ten years I've been striving to get ahead, succeed,

make it, and I'm doing it. But something is missing. I've always known it, and recently I've begun to feel as if I don't have time to do anything for anybody else. I don't even have time for myself. And then one day I was passing by this church, or a friend told me about the church, or I noticed Paul Winter was playing a concert here, or I read about your tutoring program in Bob Greene's column, and so I sneaked in on a Sunday morning and haven't missed a Sunday since. Now I want to join.

The churches have been talking and arguing for years about the apparent conflict between evangelism and social action. Evangelicals want to save souls; social activists want to save the world. Churches like Fourth Presbyterian are discovering an important secret. Sometimes trying to save the world is an important step in the direction of saving your soul. One of the consistent sources of new members is our tutoring program. It happens like this. A young urban professional comes to terms with the emptiness in his or her life, acknowledges that it has something to do with the fact that for one reason or another he or she is not reaching out to help another human being, hears about the tutoring, and decides to volunteer. The new tutor is matched with a student, tutors for a year, comes to know and care about the student, begins to feel a little better and more hopeful generally, and then one day makes a connection between what is happening personally and that place that is enabling it to happen—encouraging it, sponsoring it. They meet Jesus, even though that was farthest from their minds when the journey started, and before they know it they're sitting in an Inquirers Class and joining Fourth Presbyterian Church.

Some people come to the church in crisis. It is our job, our vocation, to meet them where they are. Some come because they have just lost a dear one, a parent, a colleague to a sudden and rapidly spreading malignancy, a partner or a friend to AIDS. Some come because they have just lost a job they assumed was long-term, and they're unemployed, full of self-recrimination, self-doubt, and fear. Some come because they are struggling with addiction. The first contact some have with church and faith is our counseling center or our social service center.

Some come because they are starting all over again in life. Having lived through the exhausting pain of divorce, they have found a new love, have remarried or plan to soon, and this time they are determined to get it right. Part of it, this time, will be faith, religion, and church. Someone has said these new church members (and I'm convinced that there are more of them than we know about) are this marvelous church's version of born-again Christians. They are, I can testify, miraculously open to the transforming power of God's love and Jesus Christ. No one hears the word of grace with as much eagerness and receptiveness as the man or woman whose life has been painfully and persistently devoid of grace.

And some, many in fact, come in strength; not because something is missing in their lives, but because a lot is right. They are "making it"; life looks hopeful; the future looks bright. They come to find a way to express gratitude and to think creatively about the meaning, for the long term, of their success.

Some come in crisis, some to start again, some in strength. All come, I believe, because they are hungry and thirsty, because they are searching for meaning and focus and a strong moral/spiritual foundation for their lives. Many talk openly of their church as their home, the congregation as their family, their return to "organized" religion as a kind of homecoming.

Professor Langdon Gilkey describes a congregation both as a "transforming community" engaged in world-changing social action and also a "rescuing community" that, like Noah's Ark, actually saves people from the storm raging outside:

> Present secular society is redolent with anxieties of all sorts; its personal sins of abuse, radical self-interest, of materialism and of greed, not only destroying individuals and families alike but overflowing into our natural environment to destroy it. People are hassled, anxious, guilty, lonely-tortured by their personal vices, their isolation from others, their impending deaths, and by the stark meaninglessness of their existence.

For all this,

> they need a supportive community, a community to rescue them from themselves, their talents, their weaknesses, their life . . . the church not as contracted community, but the church as an ark. The church where finitude, fate, sin and death are articulated, confessed and resolved through grace.[5]

Transforming, Rescuing, Supporting

We are a generation of seekers, and what we are looking for is not merely self-fulfillment, happiness, or a religious rationale for our consumer culture. The search is for authentic transformation: for a place that is different from the culture and a community where relationships are based on mutuality, compassion, forgiveness, and love.

The church has an opportunity because people are seeking what the church has and is. Those of us in the mainline churches can, I believe, be grateful for the integrity of the search, the continuing willingness of people to look to the church. We can and should, I believe, be grateful for the corrective witness of the megachurches, learn what they have to teach us, and then reclaim our own precious and lively tradition.

When I look out from the pulpit on Sunday morning at the people who have come to a traditional, mainline Presbyterian Church, I am humbly grateful. And I think of one of my favorite Psalms:

O God, you are my God, I seek you,
    my soul thirsts for you;
my flesh faints for you,
    as in a dry and weary land
        where there is no water.
So I have looked upon you in
    the sanctuary, . . .
Because your steadfast love is
    better than life,
    my lips will praise you. . . .
as long as I live.
                    (Psalm 63:1–4)

4

Three Seekers

Q.1. What is your only comfort, in life and in death?
A.   That I belong—body and soul, in life and in death—not
       to myself but to my faithful Savior, Jesus Christ . . . ."
       —The Heidelberg Catechism, *Book of Confessions* 4.001,
                                                      PC(USA)

Today's seeker is often looking for some very practical results.
The post-modern pilgrims are more attuned to a faith that
helps them find their way through life here and now. There is
something quite pragmatic about their religious search. Truths
are not accepted because someone says they are true, no matter what that leader's religious authority may be, but because
people find that they connect; they "click" with their own quo-
tidian existence.[1]
                                                   —Harvey Cox

When Jesus turned and saw them following, he said to them,
"What are you looking for?"
                                                   (John 1:38)

They come because they are searching. They come to the churches
because they have asked questions and have not received satisfactory
answers. Sometimes they come, I think, because they have tried to
avoid asking the questions and cannot. They come sometimes
because they have not found it easy to ask the questions. The questions are not new, of course. They are about the meaning and purpose of life. They are about the resources to sustain a life that is truly
alive, a fully human, participatory life in the world. They are questions about suffering and death. But finally, I believe, they are questions about something to believe in and live for and, if necessary, die
for.
      We are a generation of seekers—Baby Boomers, the ones born
between 1946 and 1964—but because there are so many and because
they have had such an unprecedented effect on all the rest of us, we
are all seekers, involved in the search.

The search is authentic. And the church shares it, allows it to transpire inside—in adult education, in worship, in sermons. The church, which offers itself not as the exclusive answer to the questions, the object of the search, but the place where the questions are asked and the search joined, this church will, I believe, be faithful and lively and more than likely filled with seekers.

"What are you looking for?" Jesus asked two disciples of John the Baptist. It is the first thing Jesus says in the Fourth Gospel. The theme continues throughout the story. There are seekers in the pages of the New Testament, as well as in our pews on Sunday morning or looking at us wistfully as they walk by our buildings or reading our brochures and newsletters and newspaper ads.

There was a time when people attended church on Sunday because it was the socially accepted and expected thing to do. Church was a good place to be seen, to make business contacts, to add devotion, morality, dependability, and piety to ones public persona. There was a time when belonging to and, better yet, actively participating in and supporting a church was a political asset, almost a prerequisite for the aspiring political candidate in some regions of the country.

Annie Dillard talks about that time and those social expectations in her 1988 memoir, *An American Childhood*. Sitting with her junior high school friends in the balcony of a Presbyterian church in Pittsburgh, Dillard recalls looking down at the business, industrial, financial, and social leaders of the city who, having partied together the night before and knowing they would head for the country club brunch as soon as the benediction was pronounced, were at the moment praying together.

In Evan Connell's provocative novel, *Mr. Bridge and Mrs. Bridge*, the rigid, structured life of midwestern, middle class culture is brilliantly portrayed. Mr. Bridge attends church with his wife on Christmas and Easter. He is barely tolerant of the pompous preacher and views the whole procedure with detached amusement.

Nevertheless, Mr. Bridge, like Annie Dillard, was in church, attending worship, for social, political, and familial reasons. Today those compelling reasons are gone or rapidly disappearing. It is not necessary today, socially or politically, to go to church. It may still be helpful for politicians and public figures to exhibit some form of religiosity—mentioning God in public utterances, adding "God Bless America" as a kind of political benediction to speeches—but perfunctory references to God no longer have to be tied to actual intentional attendance at worship, participation in the communal life, and support of the mission of an existing church.

Today, the person who shows up on Sunday morning is there because he or she wants to be there, not in order to meet social or political expectations. Some of us, those on the far side of 50, may attend worship out of habit and because of older family expectations, but not those who have experienced the liberation characteristic of the 1960s revolution from these very same social expectations. Young adults are in church for one reason only: They choose to be there—and they are on a quest.

How tragic if we accept uncritically the general cultural wisdom that young adults and members of the Baby Boomers generation are utterly secular, greedy, and committed only to their own success, gratification, and self-fulfillment—how tragic and how wrong. Far better, it seems to me, to listen to their questions and concerns, take them seriously as authentic seekers, for that is what they are.

They came of age in and lived through a time of unprecedented financial growth and equally unprecedented social individualism. The culture of the 1980s celebrated the accumulation of personal wealth, heard (and mostly believed) the notion that the fuel that drives the engines of our culture is consumerism; the more we consume the more business and industry will produce, the more wealth will be created. The necessary factor in the equation is, of course, consumerism. Therefore, it's all right to want more, to buy more, to build your life and lifestyle on the premise that fulfillment, happiness, security, peace—and whatever else it is that we all look for—will be an inevitable product of what we earn, accumulate, consume.

We almost bought it. One television beer commercial, in particular, captured the ethos of the era. A group of men are rafting through gorgeous and challenging rapids. They make camp for the night. Beautiful filets of freshly caught fish are on the grill. The men—strong, tan, handsome—sit around the fire enjoying the commonality of their brotherhood; their implicit affluence and success are reflected in their good looks, fashionably rumpled outdoor attire, their fabulously white and straight teeth, and the simple fact that they can afford this expensive wilderness adventure. Someone opens the ice-filled cooler, pulls out a cold can, and pops the flip-top. The familiar carbonated hiss is actually the first phrase of the counterpoint of consumer culture, the response to which is "It doesn't get any better than this."

We almost bought it, almost bought the notion that a good

salary, good friends, good food, good booze, and good sex add up to
the good life. Almost, but not quite. Some of the financial superstars
have fallen. As this decade comes to a close, literature and motion
pictures have begun to portray a different notion, namely, that there
is an emptiness about consumer culture and that the market forces
that create the affluence we all enjoy are not adequate as a spiritual
context for life. "It *does* get better than this," we have learned. Or
more accurately, "this," the affluence, the self-gratification, doesn't
satisfy the deepest longings and most compelling hungers of the
human soul.

Young adults are in the pews and programs of Fourth Presbyterian
Church because they are searching for meaning, purpose, values that
stand up under the assault of consumer culture, and hope for the
future. Wade Clark Roof calls them and, by association, all of us "a
generation of seekers." But so was the generation that lived in Judea
and Samaria and Galilee in the fourth decade of the first century of
the Common Era.

A Person of Character Returning

One of my favorite characters is Nicodemus, the man whose
story prompted the author of the Fourth Gospel to write the most
memorable, and most memorized, line in all literature. "For God so
loved the world that he gave his only Son" (John 3:16).

Nicodemus is one of the best characters in literature. He is the
kind of person most of us were brought up to emulate. He is successful and influential, one of a select group of seventy, the
Sanhedrin, who serve as the government, legislature, and judiciary
of Israel under Roman occupation. Nicodemus was a good man for
whom terms like duty, responsibility, and generosity were important. I see Nicodemus in Brooks Brothers pinstripes, white shirt,
wingtip shoes, briefcase in hand, *Wall Street Journal* folded under his
arm, walking briskly up Michigan Avenue from his office to a late
afternoon meeting of the board of trustees at Fourth Presbyterian
Church.

I like Nicodemus because I know his contemporary brothers and
sisters. They, and he, are people of character. A substantial human
being dwells beneath Nicodemus's classic façade. He is a reader,
keeping three or four books going at one time, some of them sur-
prisingly ambitious. He reads what *The New York Times* tells him he
ought to read, but he is also rediscovering the poetry he hasn't read

since college, and he even tries some serious theology. He notices how much religion appears in the best novels. And when he can't sleep (an increasingly frequent occasion recently that his internist assures him is common for men of his age), he has even picked up the Bible. He finds himself thinking about and asking questions he assumed he had resolved years ago: What's it all about? What's it all mean? What's going to happen to me?

I see Nicodemus in John Updike's character, Rabbit, who makes a pilgrimage through American culture in the last half of the twentieth century. I see Nicodemus as a metaphor for what happens to us midway through life, after young adulthood, somewhere in the middle years. He is secure, his retirement package is in place. But the truth is that it has been a long time since he cared passionately about anything, including his marriage. Oh, he cares about his golf handicap, but it has been a long time since an idea, a cause, an instance of human need, or even another human being has stirred him and fully engaged his imagination—made his heart beat faster and his breath come quicker. The truth is he feels his life slipping away and that makes him sad, sometimes quietly and discreetly tearful, occasionally depressed.

And so one night, after dark, when the city was quiet and he would not be seen, Nicodemus went to see Jesus. Like the young and middle-aged adults who are showing up in church on Sunday morning, Nicodemus is searching.

In his directness Nicodemus reminds me of the young urban professionals I know. He has an almost naïve innocence when it comes to nuance. He's a businessman, accustomed to charts and graphs, profit-and-loss statements, bottom lines. He's a natural literalist. "How can this be?" he asks Jesus when he hears he must be "born again."

Jesus has to lead Nicodemus away from his literalistic understanding of the image of rebirth by saying, in effect: "I didn't mean that you literally enter your mother's womb. It's just a figure of speech, a metaphor. You must be born of God's spirit. The spirit of God, which animates all life, the life-energy of creation, must be within you."

Then an interesting thing happens. The saga of Nicodemus ends, and the author of the Fourth Gospel turns, as it were, to his audience and says: "For God so loved the world that he gave his only Son, so that everyone who believes in him may not perish but may have eternal life" (John 3:16).

The Fourth Gospel, through this marvelous character, describes
the men and women who, searching, today are turning back to institutional religion. Often they come inconspicuously. At Fourth
Presbyterian Church, for instance, we are regularly distressed to discover that a woman or a man has been attending worship, sitting in
a remote corner of the balcony, not signing any of the visitor regis-
tration pew cards we supply for as long as ten years—a whole decade
of seeking. And the Fourth Gospel also suggests something of what
people are seeking for and also the nature of our ministry to them—
a God of love, a God who so loved the world as to give a son, an only
son.

God's love revealed in Jesus Christ is the heart of what the church
believes and represents. Martin Luther called it the "Gospel in
miniature." God so loved he world . . . . God loves the world and
everything in it. . . . The world, all of it, matters—inanimate and
animate, the incredibly intricate ecosystem, one-celled plant life
and loggerhead turtles, butterflies and mountain gorillas, and us,
women and men, created in God's image. God loves all of it.

One way to read Christian history is as the old story of human
inability—or unwillingness—to believe that God truly loves the
world. One way to read Christian history is as the story of all the
conditions we have added to God's love, the strings we have tied to
it, the qualifications. It can't be true, we conclude. God can't love all
of it. Part of it, maybe; our part, the good old Western civilization
part, or the Euro-American part, or the Presbyterian part, but certainly not all of it!

Sometimes we conclude that God doesn't love the world at all,
maybe offers to love it if it will act better and deserve something of
God's affection. And sometimes we have come to be convinced that
God actually dislikes the world, prefers another world that exists
beyond time and space, a world without all the messiness and ambiguity and immorality of human life.

What Jesus meant to Nicodemus and what the churches have to
offer by way of response to the searching, inquiring, and seeking of
modern men and women is God's love—God's love revealed in
Jesus Christ.

If you believe (and by belief I mean "trust") that "God so loved
the world," it changes everything. If you believe the world is God's
beloved, then the whole matter of how humankind lives within this
fragile ecosystem, oil spills, disappearing species, the hole in the
ozone layer—all become matters of high and serious morality.

If God so loves the world, then every single human life is beloved. Therefore, it is not simply imprudent and terribly shortsighted to stand by and watch a generation of urban children wasting away—literally perishing—it is a matter of high and holy morality.

Every one of us needs to know that we are loved and valued. That's why Nicodemus came to Jesus. It is why, ultimately, men and women get up on Sunday morning and come to church.

There is strong evidence from laboratory research that love is essential to life. We know that the healthiest thing that can happen to a newborn infant is to make physical contact with a human body, to feel the love of a mother and a father. The only thing we can think to do for newborn infants who are withdrawing from a cocaine addiction passed on to them by their mothers is to cradle them, hold them close, rock them, stroke them, love them. If you have been critically ill or undergone major surgery, you know how important it is to be loved and cared for.

Love imparts value. The essence of being loved is knowing yourself to be valued, valuable.

Without that, without some indication of their own value, human beings in a sense do perish. People who do not know they have value because no one ever told them spend their lives trying to establish their own value. People who have been told that they have little or no value live out that judgment with startling consistency in their relationships with others and with society at large.

Without the transforming power of love, which imparts value, abused persons are inclined to become abusive in their relationships. We know that abused children have experienced an enormous assault on their sense of self-worth and will carry those scars all their lives. We know that abused women can actually find a way, in the absence of a sense of personal value, to assume responsibility for their own abuse, to blame themselves.

We know that parents who communicate to their children that their value depends on performance, good grades, perfect behavior, or making the team can create, as a legacy, adults who are never satisfied with their own achievements, are never able to live and rejoice in life.

We know that unemployment, an increasingly common experience among middle-aged executives caught in corporate downsizing, is experienced almost entirely as a loss of personal value that results in a crisis of self-esteem and can lead to serious depression. An Employment Task Force, with a support group that meets regularly, is one of the ways Fourth Church attempts to address this distressing situation out of its faith, which is based on the redeeming idea that every individual has value because of God's love.

When poverty and racism exist together, the result can be an entire subculture in captivity to valuelessness. The child or young person or adult who lives in one of Chicago's public housing high-rises and walks every day down five flights of stairs—dark, filthy, reeking of urine—and out onto a glass-strewn sidewalk and looks up at the world all around; the thousands of others living like this—all poor, nearly all racial minorities—cannot be blamed for concluding that people who must live like this can't be worth much. And so with terrifying consistency, valuelessness becomes a tragically self-fulfilling prophecy: Children murder children; a four-year-old dies in Cook County Hospital, beaten and abused, her father unidentified and absent, her mother's boyfriend on trial for murder.

There are, as always, social and political meanings to the belief that God loves the world. And there are deeply personal meanings. The preacher makes a serious strategic error who tries to urge the people to social action, however just, until the people understand and trust and rejoice in the truth that they are part of the world God loves and that they, each of them individually, are God's beloved.

There are no more beautiful words in the world than "I love you." There is no more beautiful sound than the voice of your beloved, your child, your grandchild, your friend, saying "You are cherished. You are valuable to me. I love you."

What we Christians believe and what the church is called to proclaim, represent, and express to the world is that in Jesus Christ, God has said those most beautiful words, "I love you."

Nicodemus, a man who represents everyone who is a seeker, fades from the story after his brief conversation with Jesus. We don't know what transpired, but we do know his life was transformed because he reappears at the end of the story.

Because I have seen it happen in other lives, the lives of contemporary men and women whose search for meaning and purpose leads them to the church, I think I know what happened to Nicodemus. His life began anew, in middle age. He was born again. He found that he cared more, loved his family more, loved life more, loved God more, loved himself more, laughed and cried more, lived more— because in Jesus Christ he heard the voice of God say "I love you."

I know it happened to Nicodemus because I have seen it happen to men and women whose lives have become new and different when they hear and experience the gospel in the community of faith.

A Passive Seeker from Samaria

Sometimes the person who is searching for meaning, purpose, and hope, the seeker, is so marginalized that coming to the church is out of the question. This is a passive seeker to whom the church must in some way find a way to go. This is the person who has to be invited to church by a friend, or more likely, befriended without condition.

The biblical model of a passive seeker, the Samaritan woman Jesus meets at a well, is another compelling character in the Fourth Gospel. Hers is a fascinating story. Often when men and women in the Bible meet at a well, romance is the result. Isaac, Jacob, and Moses each find their wife at a well. It doesn't happen here—but that context comes to mind when we read the story, and it was clearly on the minds of Jesus' friends and supporters.

When the friends of Jesus return from running an errand and find Jesus sitting at a well sharing a cup of water and talking to a woman, they are startled because in their culture this is a potentially romantic and matrimonially promising situation. This woman, however, was unsuitable: She was no innocent maid, appropriate for romancing and available for marriage. Rather, she was a very compromised woman—married five times, now living with a sixth man, and worst of all, a Samaritan.

Samaria was a despicable place, according to Jewish belief and custom, and Samaritans were despicable people—all of them. It was their genes, their race, their religion. Jews thought Samaritans were racially inferior, and the contempt and animosity all went back to a religious fight two hundred years earlier about whose temple was the right one and whose religion was God's favorite. It all sounds so distressingly familiar. Out of this recognizable human matrix came a virulent racism: Those people are lazy. They don't keep themselves clean. They are not dependable. They smell funny.

The Samaritan woman was a marginal person in an already marginalized culture. Jews regarded Samaritans as inferior, women as inferior to men. In addition, this woman was flagrantly amoral, at best; immoral, at worst. Married five times and living with number six, feminist theologian Letty Russell says she has three strikes against her. She is "foreign, fallen, and female."[2]

That explains why the woman is at the well at noon, the sixth hour, in the full heat of the day. Women go to the well at dusk or early morning, never in the heat of midday, unless for some reason they can't go to the well when everyone else does—unless who you are and what you have done renders you unfit for polite company— unless going in the evening subjects you to sneers and insults from your sisters and to unwelcome and uninvited sexual harassment from men who assume you must be easy.

This is who Jesus meets and engages in conversation. Their repartee at the well has a kind of charm to it. They banter about the well, their religion, her marital status. She lies about it, but somehow Jesus already knows her situation. Then she, overcome not only by his already knowing about her but also by his kindness, his acceptance in spite of what he knows about her, concludes that she is talking to a holy man.

The disciples reenter the story and consider chiding him for speaking with an immoral woman. The woman, in the meantime, ran back to town and told the townspeople about Jesus, and many Samaritans, the Fourth Gospel reports, "believed in him because of the woman's testimony" (John 4:39).

The story of Jesus and the Samaritan woman is first of all about racism and religious prejudice, a germane topic in light of escalating racial and religious intolerance and violence in our country and throughout the world. Underlying the devastating violence in what used to be Yugoslavia is a centuries-old racial hatred, supported by a tangled web of suspicion and prejudice. Muslim fundamentalists bomb Israeli bus stations. Israeli soldiers shoot Palestinians in the back. And even here, in the United States, fundamentalist Christians bomb clinics and kill physicians, supported and justified in their violence by groups claiming to be Christian.

Professor Russell discusses the sociology and psychology of exclusivism:

> We maintain our identity "over against" other groups . . . the less sure you are the more you must have another to be over against. Persons and groups who are anxious about whether they will measure up to the cultural standards of superiority usually cut others down to their size.[3]

The simple fact is that racism arises from a character flaw and a personality deficit—not in the hated, excluded group, but in the racist. The Christian who wants to build walls or draw boundaries to keep "them" out, whoever "they" are, who transforms people with whom he or she differs theologically and ethically into an enemy, has simply missed the gospel of Jesus Christ. Christianity, expressed in wonderful New Testament stories such as this one about the Samaritan woman, is apparently radically inclusive, that is, radically willing to let God be the final judge of people's personal morality and doctrinal orthodoxy.

"God doesn't seem to care when the word needs to get out," Russell quips. The story of Jesus and the woman at the well is about God's welcome, God's hospitality. It is a set of marching orders for the church as it reaches out to men and women who are marginalized in our culture, racially, religiously, or morally. Some people don't go to church because they assume that something about themselves automatically excludes them from the family of the faithful. Nothing is more tragic than to meet someone who has already concluded that he or she is not fit for church for reasons of theology or morality, and who therefore is never exposed to the transforming power of God's love. And nothing makes me as impatient with the church as its eagerness to exclude people on the basis of our judgments about their lifestyle and morality.

The woman at the well was flagrantly immoral, according to the accepted standards of both Jewish and Samaritan culture. Nobody argues that fact. Jesus accepts her, nevertheless, as she is, doesn't scold or condemn her, offers her instead living water. And the story ends with a new beginning for her and for her neighbors.

Whatever Jesus meant when he offered the woman "living water," everybody agrees that it was the one thing necessary for life, full life, complete and authentic life. And everyone agrees that Jesus is the living water, the one thing essential for human life—the expression of God's love.

This woman and this story provide the contemporary church another model of what God's love looks like. It is a practical, down-to-earth love, expressed most eloquently not as poetry or song, but as a man sitting down to talk to a woman in the middle of the day, and in that simple act, cutting through years of racial exclusiveness and thousands of years (before and after) of moral arrogance and religious bigotry.

Sometimes a reminder is all we need: a gesture that tells a person that he or she is a beloved child of God, that there is one who loves even though nobody else seems to care. That's what the church is for, I believe: a visible, tangible reminder that each individual is loved by God.

Church should be, always, an intentional attempt—sometimes halting, sometimes inadequate, sometimes foolish—to say this to the world. There is another way to live, to be. It is God's way. It doesn't depend on or take much account of skin color, or lifestyle, or economics, or sexual orientation, or ideology. It is the way of Jesus.

The Samaritan woman, who had been married five times and was living with number six, ran home to tell others about Jesus. That's what happens when people meet Jesus. That's what the church is about.

A First-Century Young Urban Professional

The third seeker is a young man who, like Nicodemus, takes the initiative and comes to see Jesus. Like Nicodemus, he has an agenda, a question to ask, a goal to achieve. He is so like the young men and women who come to Fourth Presbyterian Church that I feel as if I know him.

He is one of the most authentic characters in the Bible. He's hard-working, successful, responsible; he volunteers some in his spare time, and he's doing well financially. But there's something missing in his life. There's an empty restlessness, a kind of permanent hunger in the pit of his soul—something T. S. Eliot described when he wrote, "we are the hollow men"; and something Arthur Miller defined poignantly in *Death of a Salesman*; and what St. Augustine meant when he wrote the truest line of all, "Our hearts are restless until they rest in thee."

And so it's a great moment when a wealthy young man runs up to Jesus, a poor itinerant rabbi, falls on his knees before him, and asks, "Good Teacher, what must I do to inherit eternal life?" What follows is intriguing and instructive for the church if we listen carefully to the dialogue in Mark 10:19–20, paraphrased below.

"Obey the law," Jesus says. "You know the commandments."

"Teacher, I do that already," the young man answers. "I've been keeping the commandments since my youth, and I still feel empty."

This man's wholesome innocence, honest inquisitiveness, and courageous vulnerability make him a very winsome character. He has all the promise of a truly great human being, a real leader. In fact, his own religion has always told him that he was living the good life by assuring him that wealth is evidence of God's blessing. So what in the world is wrong with him! Why can't he feel good about who he is and what he has?

Jesus looks at him for a long time, loves this young man, and says to him what must be the most shattering words he or any one of us, for that matter, have ever heard: "You lack one thing; go, sell what you own, and give the money to the poor . . . then come, follow me" (Mark 10:21).

Jesus didn't say that to everyone. It is his prescription for a particular person who, when he hears it, is sad. Appalled, is more like it. Sell it all—give it all away! Who could do a thing like that? Maybe some of it, maybe make a leadership gift to the capital campaign at church, maybe even seriously consider a tithe, after taxes, of course. But sell it all? Give it all up?

This story is, first of all, about money, material goods, property— a topic with which the church has an uneasy alliance sometimes bordering on a love/hate relationship. We have to have money. We need more money. But we not only hate to ask for it, we do so in a way that reveals an uncertain ambiguity, a failing not shared by the colleges, museums, and other nonprofit organizations who have become expert in the art of asking for our member's money.

Some of the church's ambiguity about money stems from the culture. Jacob Needleman, a professor of philosophy at San Francisco State University, has written a book with the engaging title *Money and the Meaning of Life*, which is receiving a lot of attention. In it he observes this:

> In no other culture that we know of has money been such a pervasive and decisive influence. In the world we now live in, money enters into everything human beings do, into every aspect and pocket of life. This is something new.[4]

Churches may not be comfortable with the topic, but the truth is that money, its acquisition and use, and its absence, has everything in the world to do with who people are, what they are doing with their lives, and why they are doing it. Besides, the churches, for better or worse, are major stockholders in the economic system. We have property, tax-free, of course. We handle money, spend it, invest it, pay it out as salaries. A wise friend of mine keeps telling me that the churches have a choice: We either have to come to terms with our relative affluence or else become poor. He's right. And if we want to communicate good news and simply raise the issues of stewardship, values, and faithful living with our people in credible ways, we have to become clearer in the way we think and talk about money and much more sophisticated in the way we ask for it. Clergy or laity who are reluctant to speak directly about money and the role it plays in our spiritual journey would do well to study, very carefully, Jesus' conversation with the young man who came to him asking about eternal life.

Not only do we modern Americans have more material wealth than anyone else in history, but we seem to want wealth more than we want anything else. But we have made, finally, an important discovery. Money doesn't make us happy or free or immortal—or even very content. In fact, the desire for and pursuit of money can be a kind of self-imposed hell, an oppressive prison.

"Sell it all. Give it all away." is a countercultural mandate. What would happen if we all did it? Collapse is what would happen—first, on a personal economic basis; and shortly thereafter, for all the institutions to which we owe money for goods and services and mortgages; and not long after that, for all the other institutions that depend on our support: churches, museums, service industries. Does Jesus actually propose that we exercise no responsibility for our families and the future of our society? Or is this his prescription only for this young man? If so, what would his prescription be for you? What would he tell you that you need to do to inherit eternal life? Would it not be different for each of us? Would he not see the issue for each one of us and name it? He would, I believe, identify whatever it is we have invested our hopes and dreams in and are counting on to save us and guarantee our security, our careers, our investment portfolios, our influence and power. He would, I think, tell us to release our grip on whatever it is that we think will save our souls, to open our hands, to let it go.

Princeton University sociologist Robert Wuthnow scolds those of us in the mainline churches who are not wrestling with this issue. Americans are asking basic questions of meaning and purpose, perhaps as never before, and the churches are failing them precisely because of the ambiguity about this issue and our lack of nerve. It is a long way, Wuthnow quips, from the pathetic pleading that most of us do over a percentage point increase in pledge commitments to Jesus' invitation to take up a cross and follow him, or to Jesus' advice to the young man to sell all and give all.

Now there is a dilemma here for those of us who live theologically and ecclesiastically in mainline churches. We are not a tight band of a few absolutely committed disciples. We appear to be "public churches," a home for the passionately devoted, the mildly interested, the occasionally curious. It would be a mistake, and

terribly presumptuous, to respond to the seeker, perhaps acknowledging her or his spiritual hunger for the first time, by suggesting
that she or he begin the process of spiritual growth by making a
generous pledge to the building fund.

And yet—and yet—I cannot shed my lifelong suspicion that part
of the crisis of religion and the churches and the crisis in our culture
is precisely ambiguity about this matter of commitment and sacrifice, our inclination, therefore, to present the gospel of Christ as a
set of ideas, opinions not substantially different from many other
available sets of opinions, one perspective for consideration out of
many, and the mission of the church as a set of modestly helpful
activities rather than a faithful representation of the one who one
day said, "Sell it all. Give it all."

This winsome young man who came to Jesus asking about eternal life represents the contemporary men and women, young urban
professionals, middle-aged executives—people of all stations and
incomes who come to church for essentially the same reason as that
young man came to Jesus: to learn what must be done to find life. I
see him in myself as well. He has succeeded professionally. He has
lived well. He has done everything his religion and his culture have
told him to do all his life. He doesn't know what else to do to produce the experience he wants to satisfy the hunger he still feels.

The radical message of Christianity is that what he, and we, most
need and want is offered to us as a gift. It is God's love, God's forgiveness, God's acceptance.

You cannot receive a gift, someone once noted, if your hands are
already full. What the gospel of Christ proposes is a different way of
living in relation to our resources, a new way of living that is intentionally unattached to all the things our culture says we absolutely
must have in order to live.

The truth inherent in the interchange between Jesus and the
young man, Jesus and us, is that we don't ultimately own anything
we cannot do without or give away. Giving away, not saving and
conserving, is the secret to the life we seek.

Annie Dillard, reflecting on her craft, wrote this:

> One of the few things I know about writing is this: spend it
> all, shoot it, play it, lose it all, right away, every time. . . . Do
> not hoard what seems good for a later time in the book, or
> for another book; give it, give it all, give it now. Something
> more will arise later, something better. These things fill
> from behind, like well water. Similarly, the impulse to keep

to yourself what you have learned is not only shameful, it is destructive. Anything you do not give freely and abundantly becomes lost to you. You open your safe and find ashes.[5]

This is not an easy lesson. Those of us on the short side of fifty have come of age in a culture of acquisition: "earn, consume, discard, earn more." Those of us on the long side of fifty were influenced, at least in part, by a very different ethos that resulted from the Great Depression, our parents' most powerful formative experience. One of our basic life scripts is "earn, save, conserve, save, protect what you have, because you never know what might happen."

The truth is that we don't own anything we cannot do without. We are in bondage to anything we cannot give away, or at least use and enjoy. And that, I think, is what Jesus saw when he looked intently at the young man who came asking about eternal life. And that, I believe, is exactly the place where the gospel intersects most powerfully with the lives of the people who attend our churches and, of course, with our own lives.

The church needs money. Sometimes it seems as if the church is always asking for money. Sometimes that indictment is true. But money is not the point, ultimately. The point is life, life now, with meaning and purpose and the fullness of eternity about it. It is what Jesus Christ came to give. It is a gift. It will belong to the person who releases his or her grip on whatever it is he or she is clasping tightly, allowing God's love, God's grace and forgiveness and new life, to fill the heart.

At the very end of Mark's account of Jesus and the rich man, his disciples, astonished at the extraordinariness of his command to sell and give all, speak for us all: "Then who can be saved?" they ask for us.

Jesus' response concludes this important interchange with a grace note: "For mortals it is impossible, but not for God; for God all things are possible" (Mark 10:26–27). A little more so, apparently, when our hands are open.

There was a time in American history when people attended church because it was the socially accepted and expected thing to do. It is not our time, this time. More and more people come to church today with a refreshing new integrity and intentionality. Instead of lamenting that there are not more of them, we should be thanking God for their presence, the authenticity and integrity of their search. They are coming because they seek meaning and purpose and, in addition, hope for themselves, for their children, for the world. They come sometimes in crisis, sometimes in despair, but oftentimes in strength. They come because they want their lives to make a difference. And they come, all of them, out of an experienced and acknowledged incompleteness, emptiness, hunger, and thirst.

Taking them and their quest seriously is the highest priority for the churches. It is exactly what Jesus did when Nicodemus came to him at night, when he encountered the Samaritan woman at the well, when the rich man asked him about eternal life. He listened, intently and deeply, to those first-century seekers; he took with utmost seriousness their concerns, questions, hungers, and thirsts; and he gave them food for their hunger and living water for their thirst. He gave them himself, of course, God's unconditional love.

It is a good time to be the church of Jesus Christ, an opportune time to proclaim and live the good news of the gospel to a world that seems newly aware of its need.

5

The Connection Is Worship

The light of nature showeth that there is a God, who hath
lordship and sovereignty over all; is good, and doeth good
unto all; and is therefore to be feared, loved, praised, called
upon, trusted in, and served with all the heart, and with all the
soul, and with all the might.
—Westminster Confession of Faith, *Book of Confessions* 6.112,
PC(USA)

Worship is at the very heart of the church's life. All that the
church is and does is rooted in its worship. The community of
faith, gathered in response to God's call, is formed in its worship. Worship is the principal influence that shapes our faith,
and is the most visible way we express the faith.
—*Book of Common Worship*, preface, p. 1, PC(USA)

A little boy, age five, was sitting with his mother in a pew in Fourth
Presbyterian Church on a Sunday morning. He was clearly
impressed with the size of the place and was taking it all in during the
prelude, neck craned to see the high ceiling with its newly lighted
beams and trusses, flanked by fourteen angels fifty feet from the
floor, each playing one of the instruments described in Psalm 150. It
is impressive space, intended to be so by its builders, the people of
Fourth Presbyterian Church in 1912, and its designers, the distinguished architects Ralph Adams Cram and Howard Van Doren
Shaw. Cram, who specialized in English gothic, agreed with the
building committee's ambitious goal to create the finest church
building in the midwest. We lay no claim to that title, but it is
impressive space, particularly as it contrasts with the bright, busy
urban intersection immediately outside.

The little boy continued to gaze admiringly at the ceiling, the
angels, and the stained glass. In a stage whisper heard for several
pews around, he asked, "Mommy, is God here?"

"Yes, dear, God is here," his mother answered.

At that moment the three clergy who would participate in leading the worship service entered the chancel through their discreet side entrance.

"Mommy," he asked, now in full voice, "is that God?"

"No, honey," she responded, loud enough that her neighbors could hear, "that's not God. Those are just the ministers."

After pondering the emerging enigma for a few moments, he asked another question: "Mommy, where is God then?"

"God is all around us."

The teller of the story reported that at this point, the organist modulated into the familiar strains, and the congregation rose to begin worship by singing the Doxology.

The little boy, as is frequently the case with our children, was asking the right questions. Is God here? Where is God? And his mother was doing her best to express one of the theological paradoxes reflected in our ideas about holy places in general and about our church buildings in particular.

God is not contained in or confined to buildings built by human hands. It is one of our foundational theological understandings. God is omnipresent; present everywhere. And yet particular spaces become spiritually and theologically significant for us. We design churches specifically to remind us of the presence of God.

To step into the sanctuary of Fourth Presbyterian Church, just a few feet away from the noisy, crowded sidewalks of downtown Chicago, is to step into a different world. The architecture itself speaks eloquently about this church's history and the fact that its past is important. The symbols that adorn the space, visible once your eyes adjust to the dimmed light, are from another era: sailing vessels, apostles, sheep, thistles, roses, bread, wine, a cross carved in stone, stained glass, and decorative wood. The music in this place likewise speaks of difference, otherness. It is music from another time, often written centuries ago, occasionally decades ago; only rarely is it contemporary music. The chief musical instrument, a pipe organ, is unique, and it is found principally in churches and only occasionally in concert halls. It is not an instrument one hears much outside the church.

The vocabulary used in this place is also uncommon. People speak of gloria patris, doxologies, homilies and offertories, preludes, postludes, and kyries. Even the attire of the people in this place contrasts dramatically with the wide range of ensembles evident on Michigan Avenue—from shorts and muscle shirts to the dark, layered, backwards-baseball-cap combination of choice among urban adolescents, to exquisite, fashionable couples on their way to an elegant cocktail party. Inside the church, people intentionally dress rather more formally than they do elsewhere, and the leaders—the clergy and the choir—are attired in robes, the ministers in black with white collar trim and two Geneva tabs.

There is a lot of misunderstanding here. It would appear that the entire project—the building, the symbols, the vocabulary, the attire—is a studied attempt to avoid or deny the fact that this is the twentieth century. And so potent are all those symbols that sometimes the church sees itself as a retreat from the world, a cloister from the city, a quiet escape to a simpler past.

The intentionally secular megachurches are a reaction to this churchy otherworldliness. New, market-wise churches intentionally do not look religious, and they avoid traditional religious architecture, music, symbols, vocabulary, and attire. These churches assume that people have simply stopped regarding traditional religion as relevant, and in order to break through to the thoroughly modern, and therefore secular, mind-set of contemporary Americans, religion must shed its traditional trappings.

We don't do that. We don't try, in fact. I am not willing to sacrifice the traditional symbols because the symbols constitute a tradition, in the case of Fourth Presbyterian Church, the "Reformed tradition." And my strong conviction is that this tradition is lively, always responsive to, and engaged in an energetically intelligent dialogue with the world. The traditional symbols are not the point. The point is to be the church in a certain way, a way that has a history, and has, over the years and centuries, learned how faithfully to live in the world.

Part of what it means to be a Protestant, particularly in the Reformed branch of Protestantism, is the commitment to continuing reformation, continuing response by the church to what is happening around it. It is a very different matter to rearrange the furniture within the church for the sake of appearing to be relevant than to stick with the old furniture because it is well built and then to be relevant in proclamation, life, and mission.

Brian Gerrish, formerly professor of theology at the University of Chicago, argues that the inclination to revise theology as a response to what is happening in the world is a part of the theology of both Martin Luther and John Calvin. Hans Küng, in his book on the Apostles' Creed, reminds us that Luther and Calvin had to know about adapting and responding intelligently to change: both of them knew about Copernicus and the literal universe-altering implications of his ideas.

My argument is that the Reformed tradition is itself lively, and it requires an intentional openness and responsiveness to the world. You don't have to attempt to be relevant within the tradition. The tradition itself, by definition, requires it.

What the tradition adds is a sense of history, a sense of belonging to a stream of faithfulness flowing out of the past. What it provides is an opportunity to join our voices for a few decades to a chorus that has been singing for centuries, since long before we were born, and that will go on singing after we die. But the tradition itself incorporates relevance because of its insistence that the world be taken absolutely seriously.

In the meantime, the high gothic sanctuary of Fourth Presbyterian Church is an awesome space, and we try to use it to communicate something of what it represents, namely, the transcendent, the presence of the holy in the secular, God at a busy urban intersection. We keep the sanctuary open from nine to five o'clock every day of the week. There are plenty of reasons to keep it closed and locked tightly. The homeless use it for warmth in winter and as a place to store their belongings in relative security while they nap in a pew. The risk of vandalism, mugging, or worse is always present. A closed-circuit television scanner allows our receptionist to keep an eye on the space, and our house staff regularly monitors it when the sanctuary is open. We believe it is important that our doors be open daily—that it says something about who we are and what we believe.

Many people come into the sanctuary every day. In addition to the homeless, tourists, oftentimes several hundred on a busy Saturday, come to take a look around. Busy urbanites stop on the way to or from work and sit quietly to pray.

Outside the sanctuary, our garth, an old English word for courtyard, is a quiet, grassy spot with two large silver maple trees, ivy, shrubbery, and a fountain in the center. Hundreds of people daily walk the few steps from the sidewalk, through the cloister, to experience a few moments of quiet. We even attract an impressive variety of songbirds and a legion of busy sparrows to sing their counterpoint to the noise of buses and taxis.

We display sculpture in the garth during the annual Festival of the Arts. We sponsor the Music on Michigan program at noon on Thursdays all summer long, featuring a variety of musical offerings—folk, jazz, classical—sack lunches, and iced tea. Sunday Night Live is another summer musical series in the garth, scheduled to precede vesper worship service. At Christmas, in addition to wreaths and the traditional tiny white lights that illuminate the entire sweep of Michigan Avenue to the delight of tourists and hundreds of thousands of Christmas shoppers, we exhibit our "electric sheep." Commissioned and created by Chicago artist John David Mooney, the four life-sized sheep are constructed out of rough lumber and strips of miniature white lights. It is impossible to walk by and not see them; they make people think, if only for a moment, about the story of a birth and sheep on the hillside as angels sang, our countercultural addition to the frenzied holiday celebration going on all around us.

We think our building is our primary instrument of interest and mission, and so we attempt to use it thoroughly and faithfully. Church buildings may be one of our society's least used assets. Church buildings ought to be open, always, for people to see and experience. In modern culture, the building itself will speak a clear and eloquent word about the faith if we simply try to be as creative as possible about its use.

The word the building speaks is not exclusively a function of size, location or grand architecture. Churches become holy space by reason of what transpires within them. In Kathleen Norris's best-selling memoir *Dakota*, the author, who had not been to church for years, started to worship at the local Presbyterian church in the South Dakota community to which she and her husband had moved from Manhattan. Norris, who eventually served the church as a supply preacher, adds a lovely, affectionate, portrait of Hope Presbyterian Church to her memoirs.

> Hope Church is an unassuming frame building that stands in a pasture at the edge of a coulee where ash trees and berry bushes flourish; chokecherry, snowberry, buffalo berry. The place doesn't look like much, even when most of the membership has arrived on Sunday morning, yet it's one of the most successful churches I know. Along with Center School, the one-room schoolhouse that currently serves nine children from Grand Valley, Riverside, and Rolling Green townships in southwest Corson County, Hope Church gives the people who live around it a sense of identity.[1]

Public Worship: The Primary
Activity of the Church

I can recall with precision what the church in which I worshiped as a child looked like. I can recall the feel of the pew cushions, the slightly musty odor, the sun streaming through the large stained-glass picture of Jesus in the garden. I can recall the people who sat all around us, my Uncle Charles and Aunt Helen on the aisle, the Crawfords immediately in front of us, and the Winters behind. I can recall staring at Mrs. Crawford's fabulous fox fur that she wrapped over her shoulders. The fox and I stared at one another for many an hour. I recall mints from my mother's purse, Dad's railroad watch that he took from his pocket and wound, a little too ceremoniously, when he decided the preacher had gone on long enough. To be alone in that space—it happened to me only once or twice as a child —was to be accompanied by an unaccountable sense of excitement—anxiety, perhaps, complete with raised hair on the back of my neck. And still, only once a decade, on the occasion when I visit and walk into that sanctuary, I know I am standing on holy ground.

What happens mostly in the space, of course, is public worship. If the lively tradition is going to connect with life in any meaningful way, it will happen as the church worships. Sometimes—often, I fear—the connection is not made. Too often I have discovered that worship in the Reformed tradition, which we wrongly assume is "nonliturgical," is dreadful, obviously unplanned, held together by not much more than the necessity of finishing up in sixty minutes, and, for my taste at least, altogether too folksy and casual.

At the risk of sounding like a curmudgeon, I'll express here my discomfort when I sit down in a pew for worship, offer up a prayer to God to ready my heart and mind for this encounter that I intend, only to have the minister stand up and say "Good morning, it's great to see you all today," as if we had just met at the grocery store or a gas station. I have come, in some way, to meet God, not the minister. The minister's job, in fact the task of everyone involved in worship, is to facilitate that encounter, which I happen to believe is a matter of life and death for me. The time to exchange greetings with the minister and my fellow worshipers will come—but not here, please, as I try to get my mind around the most incredible proposition of my life, namely, that I live in the presence of and somehow in communication with God.

It is easy of course to critique others' taste in art, music, political ideology, or worship styles. No one way, no one liturgy is right for everyone. What is necessary, I suggest, is integrity and a mutual acknowledgment that this activity we are about to engage in is, or well may be, the most important thing we will do all week. Therefore, it demands our best. It requires that those who are responsible for its conduct bring to it their very best planning, preparation, and implementation. To lead a service of public worship is to have in one's hands a very major responsibility.

We spend a lot of time at Fourth Presbyterian Church talking about and planning worship, even though our Sunday service is quite traditional and varies very little in format from week to week. We have the benefit of a staff team that includes a full-time musician to help us think about the worship life of the congregation. But the principles we use are applicable in every situation. My principles, or assumptions, about public worship are these:

Public worship is the primary activity of the church. It is by no means the only activity, but it is primary, and it is the source of the people's life together.

Public worship is an important event in the lives of the individuals who do it. The people who attend do not have to be there. They have other alternatives, some very enticing. They have chosen to get out of bed, dress up, and spend an hour or so sitting in an uncomfortable pew because worship is important to them.

Public worship is the church's opportunity to make its witness; to say what it believes and to affirm its tradition: Reformed, Presbyterian, Lutheran, Methodist, Roman Catholic, Episcopal, Baptist.

Public worship is the time the church tells the story of its faith, seasonally throughout the church year, and thus guides and nurtures the faith journeys of the worshiping community.

Public worship is the context for the proclamation of the gospel in word and sacrament, the occasion when a remarkable thing still happens: a group of people consents to sit quietly for much longer than they will agree to listen to anyone else during the week, and to listen while someone they have chosen to do the task speaks to them.

Public worship is the occasion when Christian faith and life intersect, and much of that critical encounter happens, or does not happen, in the sermon.

Those are my assumptions as I think about public worship at
Fourth Presbyterian Church. I think they are both practical and relevant for all of us who lead and engage in public worship, and from
them I believe come several guidelines, or mandates if you will, for
those who plan and lead public worship: ministers, musicians, worship committees, lay liturgists, ushers.

Because public worship is the primary activity of the church, the
source of the congregation's life, and therefore the inspiration for its
mission, and because the people who attend it have chosen to devote
several hours out of their busy lives to the activity, those who lead
must do so with energy, imagination, intelligence, and love.

It begins in the heart of the minister, I believe, with the acknowledgment, reaffirmed weekly, that leading these people in worship is
why she or he is here. It is that minister's basic responsibility, not his
or her only one, to be sure, but it is fundamental to everything else
his or her ministry encompasses. Therefore, I will bring to it my
best efforts and give it top priority.

The efficacy of a particular worship experience often depends on
what happens in the first five minutes after the worshiper arrives. It is
a matter of more importance than we realize that people be greeted
warmly and then shown how to find a place. Most already know;
many have been sitting in the same place for years! But some do not.
For the occasional visitor, the friend invited to worship, the unwary
house guest dragged along after breakfast, entering a church for the
purpose of worship is neither familiar nor comfortable. So greeters
and ushers are very important leaders. Ushers should know what
they are doing and how to do it well. In the large sanctuary of
Fourth Presbyterian Church individuals have been serving as ushers
for particular sections of the sanctuary for years. They know the
people who sit in their section by name; the people become "their"
people, and ushers, in a very significant sense, become ministers to
small communities within the larger congregation. Regardless of a
church's size, however, what happens between individuals in the
first few minutes will influence the entire experience.

The bulletin containing the order of worship and other necessary
information for the life of the community is the first thing the worshiper sees. Is it attractive, neat, user-friendly? Does it communicate
not only by the information it contains but by the way it is format-
ted and edited that this is a very important hour in the life of the
community? The bulletin could include a prayer for preparation for
worship—the prayer of the day from the Book of Common

Worship, for instance, or a thoughtful sentence or two that relates to the sermon theme or the theme of the entire service.

Music and Worship

The musical prelude is not simply background music to cover the noise of the people's gathering and greeting one another. It is a prelude to worship. The music itself is important. I have had extraordinarily pleasant relationships with all the musicians with whom I have been privileged to work. Each of them—particularly my former colleagues, Elizabeth Lange at the Broad Street Presbyterian Church of Columbus, Ohio; Dr. Morgan F. Simmons, who served at Fourth Presbyterian Church as organist/choirmaster for twenty-seven years; and my current colleague, John Sherer—have been open to my thoughts, more than eager to work together, and happy for my input as they have planned the music for worship. The prelude sets the tone inviting worshipers into God's presence. Often the prelude begins with the strongest, liveliest composition, moves gradually to quieter, more devotional works, and concludes when all the people are in place and the service itself is about to begin, with the organ playing softly—beautifully, to be sure—but very softly. I argue that the opening of worship on most Sundays of the year, an act of utter praise and adoration of God, should be lively, strong, and occasionally absolutely thrilling. It follows, I reason, that the organist should offer the strongest composition last, letting out all the stops on occasion, suggesting musically for the now wide awake worshipers that something very interesting is about to happen.

Music is absolutely essential to worship. We turn to art to help us express what we can never quite adequately define with words. The relationship between our particular religious traditions and the arts has not always been a happy one. Zealous reformers ripped out the statuary and carved rood screens from their gorgeous cathedrals, whitewashed the walls, installed clear glass in the windows, and even banned pipe organs or the singing of anything other than Psalms. The power of that liturgical revolution is at the heart of the Reformed and Presbyterian tradition, but happily some of its excesses have been moderated, and we are returning to a healthier and more creative relationship with the arts.

We are finally acknowledging, once again, that the arts and religion are often up to the same things, reaching for the transcendent, celebrating the depth and mystery of life, affirming that holiness is occasionally beautiful, and furthermore, that what we experience in an encounter with the arts can be and often is an authentic spiritual event or religious experience. I know what that means when I stand humbly before the mysterious splendor of Vincent Van Gogh's *Starry Night*, or see Claude Monet's *Water Lilies* or Georgia O'Keeffe's magnificent *Irises*, or view the raw power of Picasso's *Guernica*. I have never been able to deny the depth of my own experience sitting in a concert hall and feeling a lump in my throat and tears in my eyes at the glory of Beethoven's Ninth Symphony, or the passion of Samuel Barber's Adagio for Strings, or the energy of a Mozart string quartet, or the delicacy of a Handel soprano and trumpet aria.

The more I open my spirit, the more I experience the awesome depth and mystery of existence—in the poetry of W. H. Auden, Wendell Berry, May Sarton, John Updike, and Gwendolyn Brooks, and in the bold lines and strokes of Frank Lloyd Wright's architecture or the stimulating and challenging symmetry of Chicago's skyline. It is not possible, I think, to miss the meaning and the theological truth of the parable of the prodigal son when it is danced by a ballet virtuoso such as Edward Villella, or to miss the profound pathos and tragedy of untimely death as Juliet cradles Romeo's lifeless body in the stunning conclusion to Prokofiev's ballet.

The arts, Presbyterian theologian Theodore Gill has taught us, are windows opening into transcendence. And I have always known it, long before I had words to describe it, when I stood to sing one of these great hymns of praise at the opening of public worship: "Praise to the Lord, the Almighty," or "Holy, Holy, Holy," or "Joyful, Joyful, We Adore Thee." And now, we enjoy some wonderful new hymns like "Earth and All the Stars" and "God Is Here."

People who attend worship tell us how important music is. Over the years I have had far more complaints about my choice of hymns than about the content of my sermons. An inherent tension exists between what people want to sing and enjoy singing and what ministers and musicians think they ought to sing. That tension is exacerbated now by the possibility of introducing some of the wonderful new hymns that have been written recently or using newly accessible hymns from other traditions.

The topic, and the choices we make, require thoughtfulness, sensitivity, and creativity. No one wants the congregation to go home angry because of the hymns they were forced to sing! At Fourth Presbyterian Church we try to start and/or end with something we know people enjoy singing—a strong, familiar hymn tune. There must always be one familiar hymn in the service, preferably two, but people are open to diversity if hymns reflect the service theme, for instance. And almost everyone will agree to an effort to learn new hymns by introducing a "hymn of the month," sung first by choir or soloist, followed by the congregation, and accompanied by information in the bulletin about the composer and the author.

Music is one of the most obvious ways the church intersects with the world. Our music tradition is an excellent one, but it is imperative that we not confine ourselves rigidly to it. Regardless of our expertise, we can all sing an African-American spiritual or listen to a jazz group making a joyful noise to the Lord.

The Spoken Word

Because worship is important to the people who attend it, and because it is the church's opportunity to speak publicly about the Christian faith, every element of the service should be planned with great care and creativity. If the minister or worship leader stumbles over the pronunciation of a name in the Old Testament lesson or fails to negotiate the awkward punctuation or verse division of the responsive readings, the people may conclude that this is the first time he or she has read the text or even thought about reading to and for the congregation. Nothing communicates the importance of worship as clearly as the thoughtful preparation—or its absence—by the leader.

Leaders should practice. Every word that will be said out loud in worship should be practiced before the service. Leaders should attend regularly to basic reading and speaking skills, not to make a dramatic production out of worship but in order to be heard.

I have long been wary of spontaneity in worship leadership. As a youngster I used to attend a Baptist church with my neighborhood pals on Sunday night. It was interesting and lively, and the girls were pretty. At the end of each Baptist Young People's Union (BYPU) meeting, we would sit in a circle and pray; the prayers were to be spontaneous. This was something of a new and frightening experience for me, so I listened carefully to what my friends were saying. I noticed quickly that they said essentially the same thing to God week after week. It was no great trick to pick up the phrases and words, and I became an acceptable prayer myself. Then I noticed that in the adult all-church prayer meeting that followed, the same thing happened. The same phrases, over and over, were invoked by many of the same people. My friends had encouraged me to let the Spirit lead my spontaneous prayer, but the Spirit seemed to be in something of a rut when it came both to topics and to the words used to express them. So I came to a conclusion that has served me well: Spontaneity can serve as a disguise for not being prepared. Unwritten prayers, intended to come from the heart, come instead from our mental warehouse of stock phrases and are almost invariably monotonously repetitious.

The minister has no greater or more serious pastoral responsibility than to offer the Prayer of the People, the pastoral prayer, in public worship. We hope the praying will gather up something of what is happening in the lives and hearts of worshipers, express for everyone what they need and want to say, and at the same time, remain open to Paul's amazing assumption that the Spirit prays in us with "sighs too deep for words." The Prayer of the People requires thoughtful preparation, and it is informed by the theology of the church and the life of the community. It must be written beforehand, either in manuscript or outline. It should be prepared after the sermon is written so that homiletical themes can be deepened in the hearts and spirits of worshipers. And it, too, because it is public speech on one level, must be rehearsed and critiqued.

I am regularly moved by the prayers of my colleagues in worship. Their thoughtful prayers allow me to pray. My colleagues become my pastors in a powerful way as they speak to me and for me in their prayers. It is a special gift, and it happens because they prepare carefully.

It was the theologian Søren Kierkegaard who gave us the metaphor of theater for worship. People come to worship, he maintained, with the same expectations they bring to a night at the theater: They expect that something will happen to them and that they will be entertained, induced to laugh or cry. They come as audience to hear the actor (preacher) and supporting cast (choir), and they hope God will serve as the prompter.

We have it backward, Kierkegaard maintained. Worship is theater, to be sure, but the people of the congregation are the actors. The clergy and musicians are prompters, and God is the audience.

No, worship is not a drama for the congregation's entertainment. But yes, it is theater, an act performed by a community that intends to worship God. Theater requires preparation, room for spontaneity—but always with structure, rhythm, and a script.

Public worship becomes boring when we forget the basics. When details are ignored, we do things like stumble through the announcements or allow so much dead space between the different elements of the act that the whole exercise simply dies from lack of energy. Why, after all, do clergy sit down between hymns and prayers? Why the long, pregnant pauses? Are we afraid that the people who are accustomed to twenty-second soundbites of information on television can't keep up with us?

Intersecting with the World

Worship is the time and place when the church, with its theological tradition, intersects with the life of the world. On a recent Sunday morning as I sat in the chancel thinking, reflecting, and praying in preparation for worship, I was struck by the way the sounds of the city played a kind of counterpoint to the lovely J. S. Bach chorale the organist was playing. The doorman at the Four Seasons Hotel was hailing cabs across the street, and his whistle insistently sounded, its shrill upper-register blasts piercing our open windows. At the stoplight on Michigan Avenue a car waited, its deep, thudding bass woofers pounding rhythmically for all, blocks around, to hear and feel. A few feet away, audible through the south transept windows, the street musician who plays his bongo drums all day had started to work. And the first ambulance of the hour hurtled by, its siren shrieking above all the other street noises, on its way to Northwestern University Hospital's emergency room.

On our corner you can't avoid the city—the realities of life in the city—even if you want. We could, of course, try to soundproof our building, and that metaphorically is what we sometimes try to do with our churches: to make them safe, secure, impenetrable by the life of the world outside. To the degree that we do that, we are unfaithful, not very interesting to anybody, and probably slowly dying.

The place where the encounter between faith tradition and the life of the world happens most consistently is in the sermon. For Presbyterians, preaching is critical. It is not the only thing that happens in worship, but for most of us it is the critical thing, the act with which we have been identified ever since John Calvin took to his lectern and pulpit and delivered two- and three-hour homiletical marathons once or twice a day in sixteenth-century Geneva. Presbyterians have been known to refer to going to church as "going to hear Mr. Smith or Ms. Jones this morning." Preaching is a clear priority for us.

Preaching: Discipline, Process, Vocation

This is not a book on preaching. There are plenty of those, and I read them all. But I cannot discuss the life of the church in the city without at least a few brief reflections on the ministry of preaching. First and most important, preaching is the minister's vocation. I have argued here that leading the people in worship is the minister's fundamental task. And particularly for those of us who live in the Presbyterian tradition, preaching is at the heart of the worship experience. A common lament made by clergy who must preach weekly is that they never have enough time to prepare sermons adequately. There are so many demands on their time—calls to make, meetings to attend, committees to organize, leaders to recruit, and programs to launch—that the time to do serious and sustained Bible study, reading theological and literary source materials, outlining and writing, simply doesn't exist. So ministers are forced to prepare sermons on the run or in the few empty spaces in busy weekly schedules.

A friend of mine told me that he doesn't even try to think about the sermon until Saturday night other than to choose a text and title, which we all know must be identified in time to meet the bulletin printing schedule. After dinner on Saturday, he kisses his wife and children, heads over to the church, produces a sermon over the course of the night, and finishes out the torturous experience by catching what sleep he can stretched out on a pew. It works for him, and I know for a fact that his people are grateful for the integrity of his preaching. But I am sorry that he hasn't enjoyed anything resembling a normal Saturday night with his wife, children, or friends for years, and I cannot imagine the emotional burden he carries all week long, knowing what lies ahead on Saturday night.

I have engaged in the traditional lament of the busy, over-committed clergyperson about not having enough time to prepare sermons. I still do regularly. But I also regularly remind myself that the congregation that called me to be its pastor expects me to preach and that people are coming on Sunday morning hoping to hear a word from the Lord in the sermon I offer. I regularly remind myself of the incredible privilege and burden of this arrangement. These people are paying me to do this. I frequently recall Fred Craddock's image of the people paying the preacher to go to the study, the scripture, for them each week, to inquire on their behalf, and then to bring to Sunday morning what he or she has discovered.

What the task requires is a weekly discipline based on a deep personal commitment to this task as the most important part of my ministry. The details differ for each of us, and there are many clergy whose ministries are vitally important and productive but who do not preach regularly. But for me, the discipline includes setting aside blocks of time during the week that are simply inviolate, in a place that is quiet, inaccessible except in an emergency. I have always done my most productive reading, thinking, and writing in the morning, so that is when I do my sermon work. I begin each day in my study with a thermos of coffee and the books and materials I need. Sometimes I work an hour or two or three. I write a manuscript on Thursday morning, so I remain closeted until it is completed, usually around noon.

I find that a sermon needs time to grow and emerge, and so the process does take all week. "Fermentation time," I call it. Monday is for scripture exegesis; Tuesday and Wednesday, for assembling ancillary supportive material, book references, articles, essays, notes I have collected beforehand. At the end of the Wednesday morning session I hope to have a notion of where this project is going, a kind of flow of ideas that can become an actual outline but usually does not. Thursday is for writing and typing. On Friday I read it over and begin to adjust, edit, rearrange, and change. Saturday I generally ignore it—let it "rise and bake," to mix my metaphors. Sunday I rise early, head for the pulpit, and preach it to an empty sanctuary—a very critical part of the whole process—to hear, for the first time, what the words sound like in the space the people will soon occupy. Then it's back to the study for final refinements and revisions and sometimes an entirely new conclusion or introduction. By that time, obviously, the manuscript is in my memory bank, and though I take it with me into the pulpit (a security device from which I have never freed myself), I do not depend on it much.

The details can vary for any of us, but the weekly discipline is the way I have learned to express my personal commitment to the importance of the task of preaching. It also has allowed me the wonderful luxury of spending my Saturdays and Saturday nights—the ones without wedding responsibilities at least—with family and friends.

There are two additional elements to this discipline that I find helpful. Twice a year I find a way to spend enough time in serious study to do some long-range planning. I customarily use the morning hours of summer vacation and another week or two in January for this purpose. Since the ecumenical lectionary has reemerged to guide the yearly rhythm of preaching, I read and summarize in a sentence or two each of the assigned lectionary texts for six months in advance. Then I ponder the entire half-year sweep of the lectionary to see whether major themes emerge for me. I attempt to assign a theme or motif to each Sunday, and I carefully record in my looseleaf notebook, a page for each Sunday, the scripture text for the day and whatever theme I have chosen. That discipline allows me to do two things. I can share what I have produced with the organist and choir director for their advance planning. And, most important of all, deciding on and recording a theme for each week is, for me, the equivalent of opening a file. As I read, attend motion pictures, sporting events, and concerts—that is, as I live my life—references and experiences suggest themselves around the themes I have chosen and I record them in my notebook. When the system works, the page is full when I turn to it each Monday morning and begin to work on the text.

I commit myself to attending to the lectionary as part of my responsibility to the church ecumenical. I also elect not to use the assigned texts when I feel called, inspired, or moved in another direction. I conclude that it is, for me at least, an appropriate balance between the mixture of liturgical and free church traditions within historic Presbyterianism.

The second discipline that I have found helpful, and utterly enjoyable, is reading. I was blessed to grow up in a home where both my parents, high school graduates, read constantly and voraciously: newspapers, magazines, novels, history, poetry. I grew up with the Sunday *New York Times* strewn throughout the house and several novels open on the tables and chairs. From my mother and father I learned to love words, books, writing, and reading. And so I read, intentionally, as much as I can. I have come to conclude that reading is one of the best ways to stay in touch not just with what is happening in the intellectual culture but with what is in the minds and hearts of the people who come to church on Sunday morning.

There are no fewer than six bookstores within one block of Fourth Presbyterian Church. Many of the people who attend worship read a lot. In spite of television, we are a literate people. The preaching clergyperson must know what is being written and read by the American people, the larger intellectual and spiritual currents the literature describes. Being a part of the congregation's intellectual universe is a prerequisite for preaching in a way that will be "heard" on Sunday morning.

The Sermon

I like to think of a sermon as an event that brings together, like a busy intersection, five avenues:

1. the text, studied in its context
2. the theological tradition: what the scholars have said about the subject
3. the life of the world: what history, literature, the arts have said
4. the life of the particular congregation, the particular experience of the particular people
5. the faith and experience of the preacher

The fifth avenue, the faith and experience of the preacher, is absolutely critical. Most of what I know about preaching I have learned by listening to other preachers. From James Forbes, the powerful preaching minister of Riverside Church, I learned that sermons are effective only to the degree that they are, in some way or another, the personal testimony of the preacher. If what we say is not powerfully and transformationally true for us, its truth will not be evident to those who hear us preach.

Listening to Forbes preach and teach, I had to unlearn a style of preaching I picked up in the 1960s: preaching as an objective process of intellectually discerning the word in a text and communicating that word to the intellects of the hearers. Never, never, I had learned, was my personal, subjective experience to interfere with this highly cerebral process. It was a defining moment when I realized, by listening to James Forbes, that if I don't believe it, they won't either. If in some way I am not willing to stake my life or give my life away on the basis of what I am saying, the congregation is not going to be helped much by it.

And so, in the busy intersection that is a sermon, stands the preacher, offering his or her faith experience, sharing as much as is necessary without becoming maudlin, embarrassed, or manipulative or without inviting congregational voyeurism—offering to God, week after week, his or her faith, hope, love, and trust.

In public worship, and in the preaching of sermons, my aspiration is that the people of the congregation will hear, understand, and experience these things:

The presence of God in the midst of the life of the world, the
mystery of the holy in the ordinary, by and in an act of
praise and adoration.

The reality of sin, the knowledge that things are not all right
in the world, an understanding of the distance between
what God created us to be and who we actually are.

The miracle of grace, that in spite of who we are and how often
we fail to live up to God's expectations, God loves us still
and invites us to the table and welcomes us home as beloved
children.

The "therefore" of responsibility, the element of personal
responsiveness that completes the experience. Because we
are, individually, children of God, loved, forgiven and
accepted by God, there is work to be done, mission to be
offered, responsibility—for our personal lives, our interper-
sonal relationships, our communities and our world—to be
joyfully accepted.

Week after week, in every community in our nation, Christians
engage in countercultural, and sometimes culturally subversive,
activity: They gather in their churches to affirm their belief in God,
to pray and think together about what it means to live in God's
world as God's children, and to give generously of their lives and
resources to support the work they believe God wants done in the
world.

Cynthia Campbell, president of McCormick Theological
Seminary, who is regularly in the worship congregation of Fourth
Presbyterian Church, says that it is an astonishing moment when in
the midst of the busiest, most glamorous, most aggressively materialistic neighborhood in the country, a congregation of 1,500
Christians rises and, as one, with no liturgical inducement, says, "I
believe in God the Father Almighty, maker of heaven and earth . . ."

It happens wherever Christians gather for public worship.

6

The Trajectory of Faith: Beginning with Grace

In each time and place there are particular problems and crises through which God calls the church to act. The church, guided by the Spirit, humbled by its own complicity and instructed by all attainable knowledge, seeks to discern the will of God and learn how to obey in these concrete situations.
—The Confession of 1967, *Book of Confessions* 9.43, PC(USA)

Loving us still,
God makes us heirs with Christ of the covenant.
Like a mother who will not forsake her nursing child,
like a father who runs to welcome the prodigal home,
God is faithful still.
— -A Brief Statement of Faith, *Book of Confessions* 10.3, ll. 47–51, PC(USA)

The liberal religious legacy calls the church to deeper forms of religious experience . . . . Being an eyewitness is not enough. One must become a heart-witness. . . . The fire of the Holy Spirit must burn in liberal hearts the feeling of God's forgiving love, which Graham Greene described in a reverberating phrase, The . . . appalling . . . strangeness of the mercy of God.[1]
—Leonard Sweet

On October 13, 1992, a little boy was killed in Cabrini-Green. It is one of the shameful realities of city life that children die all the time from a variety of causes—abuse, neglect, but mostly as a result of gunfire. One of the most powerful worship experiences I have ever had was to participate last year at Christmas in a memorial service for Chicago's slain children, at the Episcopal Cathedral of St. James on the Feast of the Holy Innocents, the occasion to remember Herod's slaughter of the children of Bethlehem in his effort to eliminate the boy Jesus. We don't pay much attention to that blunt tragedy in the midst of our Christmas and year-end festivities. The power of the event was heightened, for me, by the fact that I had left my three beautiful and relatively secure grandchildren playing with their new Christmas toys under the watchful and loving, attentive eye of my wife to participate in a memorial service for sixty-one Chicago children—most of them poor, most African-American, most residents of the projects, most killed by gunfire.

The little boy who was killed on October 13, 1992, was seven years old. His name was Dantrell Davis. He was shot in the head by a sniper who fired from the top floor of one of the Cabrini-Green highrises as Dantrell walked to school, hand in hand with his mother. The man who shot him used a military-style, rapid-fire rifle, complete with a highly efficient telescope sight mechanism. He said he thought he was shooting at a rival gang member. The people of Chicago were stunned. State and national newscasts carried accounts of the shooting.

Chicagoans, including the Christian community, realized as they looked at Dantrell Davis's cherubic face in his school picture in the newspaper that human life is not worth much in our city. In a moment of terrible clarity the city understood it had not only lost the war on drugs that government bravely declared a few years ago but that now an epidemic of drug using and drug dealing is occurring just a mile or two from the fashionably affluent shoppers at Bloomingdales, that the enormous profits resulting from drug traffic have fueled a resurgence of gang activity structured around the drug economy. This time, thanks to the refusal of society to commit itself to reasonable gun control, the gangs are well armed, far better armed, in fact, than officers of the Chicago Police Department. The gun that killed Dantrell Davis was not manufactured to protect citizens in their homes, to hunt squirrels, or to practice target shooting. It is the deadliest, most efficient weapon we can produce. Its purpose is to kill people, as many as possible, and as quickly and efficiently as possible. It and weapons like it—semiautomatic rifles and hand guns—are the weapons of choice among Chicago gangs.

In the aftermath of Dantrell Davis's death came a flurry of official handwringing. Politicians—local, state, and federal—made pronouncements, visited the projects, and announced new initiatives to deal with the root causes of urban violence, poverty, and unemployment. Passionate sermons were preached from pulpits around the city, including the one at Fourth Presbyterian Church.

So far as I can see, however, nothing much has happened. A few buildings have been demolished and their residents relocated. Life at Cabrini-Green goes on. A gang truce was arranged and, in fact, the level of gang violence decreased markedly at Cabrini. But most of the highrises are still there. They are still shamefully undermaintained. The elevators still don't work, and the halls still reek of urine. Unemployment and poverty and absolute family breakdown are still rampant.

A year after Dantrell Davis died, the news reported another ghastly story of a five-year-old youngster who was dropped to his death from a fourteenth-floor window at Ida B. Wells complex. His older companions had dropped him because he refused to steal candy for them.

How can we live in the city when that sort of thing happens? How can we exist a few blocks away from a place where children are gunned down or dropped from windows? Those are the moral questions that confront city people and, by extension, all people in our culture.

We have a number of alternatives. One way, of course, is to shut it out, not attend to it, not think about it. It is simply too awful to contemplate. Another way is to raise the barriers of racism and economic bigotry and conclude that it is an ethnic matter, that poor people don't have to live like that if they choose not to. Another alternative is to give in to despair and cynicism, to give up hope that things can ever be different for poor city children. This, by the way, is what happens to the children themselves, who later join gangs because there are no reasons to hope. Gangs offer structure, community, affection, and money. Who could resist?

Grace Is an Alternative

There is another alternative, and I believe the churches are its chief custodian, proponent, and interpreter. This option is to put what happens in the city in the context of the gospel we believe; to engage what happens to and within our communities with the realism of a gospel that knows about sin, but also with the hopefulness of a community that trusts in the good news and the reality of resurrection. There is a Christian word that desperately needs to be spoken about the value of every human life, the amazing grace of God in Jesus Christ that reaches out to each individual. And there is a consequent word that equally desperately needs to be heard about the redemptive possibilities, the hope, when men and women who know themselves loved by God begin to act like children of God by taking responsibility for their lives and the life of the community.

A remarkable thing happened after Dantrell Davis's murder. *Chicago Tribune* columnist Bob Greene, who lives in the neighborhood of the church, wrote about the tragedy in his popular column. He expressed the question everybody was asking: "What can I do to help." Instead of wringing their hands and giving up in despair, Greene suggested that his readers telephone Fourth Presbyterian Church and volunteer to help with the tutoring program. In the next seventy-two hours we received sixteen hundred telephone calls, swamping our receptionists and our phone systems. We recorded each name and told them that we would get back to each as soon as we could. Fourth Presbyterian Church can't use two thousand new tutors!

So we called a community meeting on a Saturday morning and invited each person who had telephoned the church to attend. We also invited people from other tutoring programs and a variety of social service and literacy projects that depend on volunteers to attend. Several hundred people, again most of them young urban professionals, showed up. We thanked them for their interest and then referred them to the variety of agencies who need volunteers, including our programs. As a result, several hundred new volunteers went to work in the city, and although I know the problems not only are not resolved but have in many ways become more tenacious— more drugs, more guns—nevertheless, I saw in that modest response a reason for hope. And the church is its custodian and proponent.

The two words we have to say to the city are about grace and responsibility. The grace note is there from the beginning. Human beings are created in God's own image, placed on the earth to do God's work. Even when we break the fundamental rules of our garden paradise and are escorted outside into human history to work and live, love and die, God is taking care of us, still sewing garments to protect, comfort, and sustain us.

Theologians have always known that the anthropological question is a theological question. Both John Calvin and Karl Barth, four centuries apart, wrote that the question of God is also, at the same time, the human question.

It's amazing how frequently this issue emerges in literature. Novelist Ernest J. Gaines has written a remarkable little book, *A Lesson before Dying*, in which a young black man named Jefferson is on trial for a murder he did not commit. The story begins in a courtroom in a small Louisiana town in 1948. The public defender assigned to the case does not even bother to argue the young man's innocence because it is a foregone conclusion he will be convicted. Instead, the attorney argues that Jefferson—poor, illiterate, black—is not quite human. Execution is not appropriate, he argues: "Gentlemen, be merciful . . . why, I would just as soon put a hog in the electric chair as this."[2]

Jefferson's grandmother, who has raised him and loves him, is determined that the public defender's description of the young man will not stand. If he dies, it will be as a man, and the symbol of his manhood, his humanness, is that he will learn to read and write. And that he does. Gaines's powerful novel concludes with Jefferson's writing a note: "tell them [the African-American community] that I'm strong, tell them I'm a man."

There are and always have been competing answers to the question of who and what we human beings are. We are products of subconscious drives, formed in us by our relationship with our parents, say some.

No, say others, we are really the simple product of a preprogrammed DNA structure that leaves little room for freedom of will and choice.

Actually, say the evolutionists, we are really the most recent product of the survival of the fittest—the primate who stood up, picked up a rock, and hurled it at his enemy.

We are body counts to some and statistical trends to others. To both Marxists and free-market capitalists, we are economically determined, essentially consumers in our market system, easily manipulated into wanting, then needing, then working hard to be able to produce and consume almost anything from automobiles to after-shave lotion.

There is, in this marketplace of answers to the human question, one more answer. It is expressed in that first story in the Hebrew scriptures, as God creates human beings, breathes breath into them, blesses them, and talks to them. These creatures are different, the scripture story maintains. They are beings who can think, plan ahead, worry, argue, complain, fuss, and walk out the door, if they choose.

"What a piece of work is man," Shakespeare wrote in *Hamlet* (act 2, scene 2). And centuries before, the psalmist said this:

> When I look at your heavens . . . the moon and stars . . .
> what are human beings that you are mindful of them? Yet
> you have made them a little lower than God, and crowned
> them with glory and honor.
>
> (Psalm 8:3–5)

"Crowned with glory." That is what scriptures say we are. That is the first and fundamental word about us, a word of grace.

The problem is that we forget it—we forget our glory as children of God. Religion ought to remind us, but the unfortunate impression many people carry away of religion's estimation of their humanity is entirely negative. Church, for many, is where they learned to think negatively about themselves. Church is where people learned to think of themselves as bad, as faulty goods, inadequate, helpless, and hopeless. Church is about sin, sin defined not only as doing bad things or thinking bad thoughts, many of them sexual, but also as pride, egotism, thinking too highly of ourselves. I believe that more people than we will ever know have left the church, and now avoid church, because their experience of the church is its judgmental, guilt-inducing, obsessive concentration on sin and the consequent negative hopeless and helpless image of humanity.

Sin is, indeed, part of our answer to the question of humanity. But it is not the only part. What is original about us, scripture suggests, is not our sin but our glory. What is fundamental about humankind is not God's condemnation but God's grace.

I've always been intrigued by the idea that if we sin by thinking too highly of ourselves, perhaps the reverse is also true; perhaps we also sin by not thinking highly enough of ourselves, forgetting who we are, denying our original glory, refusing to be the full, strong, responsible women and men God created us to be.

Plenty of forces are at work in the world to deny the glory of our humanity. In our culture there is a sense that you are a valuable human being only to the extent that you prove yourself to be. There is a sense that you are or will be respected, appreciated, even loved, if you get good grades, win, succeed, get ahead, earn a big salary, end up at or near the top; that is to say, you succeed if you live up to the expectations of others. Sometimes others' expectations are helpful and inspiring and do motivate us to stretch far more, reach higher, and work harder; but sometimes they are unreal, unreachable, and therefore cruel and oppressive. Love sometimes seems to be conditional—you get it if you earn it. When you buy into the idea (and who doesn't, at least minimally?) life becomes a proving ground, a contest to be good enough, popular enough, successful enough.

I see this attitude among many of the hard-working, success-oriented, highly motivated young urban professionals who take a breather from their busy lives by sitting in the pews of Fourth Presbyterian Church on Sunday morning. They are working hard, much harder, I believe, than anyone has before them. They are going to work before dawn, coming home after dark, six and seven days a week. Some of them bring briefcases to worship in order to head out for the office immediately after the benediction. Some of them are accomplishing their goals, and they feel good about themselves. Many understand the emptiness and loneliness of a life totally invested in the workplace. And many are falling behind, according to their own or others' expectations. They are not receiving the promotions or raises they hoped for and are feeling not only bad but guilty. And some are not working; they are losing jobs, are unable to find work, and are concluding that there is something radically wrong with themselves, some character deficit. Sometimes they retreat from relationships, stop reaching out to friends, even withdraw from the church.

Therapists are telling us that when you buy into the "personal-value-depends-on-success" syndrome, addiction and other unhealthy behavior can result—a lifestyle designed and structured to earn affection, acceptance, and love and a sustained inability to accept, value, and love yourself. The antidote, say the therapists, is steady, unconditional love—love that is based not on what you accomplish or perform, what you look like, or how much you earn, but on something about your very being, something intrinsically valuable—something like grace.

Assaults on Humanity:
Aging, the Physically Challenged, Racism

Aging, and ageism, is a force that denies the humanity of men and women in tragic ways. Life in the city is not easy for the elderly. But one of the delightful discoveries I have made is the fierce independence, determination, and strength of people who have been living in the city for years and have no desire to retire to the serenity and security of suburban geography, or to many of the available retirement facilities.

I am fascinated to observe women and men in their eighties and nineties, dressed for Chicago's legendary winters, walking several blocks through a near gale to worship on Sunday morning. One of our elderly saints, Anna Spransy, lived in the neighborhood of the church for fifty years. Born and raised in the south, in another era, she was a woman with charm, wit, and a twinkle in her eyes. When we would telephone Anna to make an appointment for a Fourth Church pastor to visit, she customarily told the minister in her southern drawl to come after 4:30—in time for sherry! One night a burglar somehow made it into her apartment and startled her after she had gone to bed. He told her he wanted her jewelry. She explained calmly that her jewelry was locked in a drawer.

"Open it," he said.

"I'll have to get out of bed to do that," she replied, "and, young man, I'm not about to get out of bed in my nightgown in front of you. So if you'll step outside for a moment, I'll open the drawer, crawl back under the covers, and you can have my jewelry."

The obviously nervous intruder did what Anna told him to do; he stepped through the door from the bedroom and onto the fire escape. Anna calmly left her bed, shut and bolted the door, stranding the young man on the fire escape. Then she called the police.

The late theologian Joseph Sittler, of the University of Chicago Divinity School, thought and wrote a lot about aging. Shortly before he died, Sittler was interviewed on the topic of aging by *Second Opinion*, The Park Ridge Center's journal on health, faith, and ethics. He responded by telling about a recent invitation to speak to the residents of a local nursing home, recipients of what Sittler liked to call "shuffle board geriatrics".

"Keep 'em happy; keep 'em sedated by entertainment; teach 'em bridge or poker; take 'em on a bus trip." And then the officially retired but still vigorously working and teaching theologian reflected: "Social science misses the internal aspects of aging: loss of identity, loss of memory, loss of role. The first thing you say to someone, after meeting them is 'What do you do?' Well, when you don't do anything any longer in American society, who are you? You're the residue of ruin."

So Sittler, who was almost totally blind at the time, tried an experiment.

> I remembered them back to identity. I told them that as I talked about my youth I wanted them to think about their own youth. So I talked about the days when I was a little kid in southern Ohio. These old people started to cry, but it was not from grief. They went out of the room talking to one another as they had never talked before. It was a recovery.[3]

What Professor Sittler helped them recover, of course, was their identity, something of their original glory. He was, for them, an agent of God's grace.

We are working hard at Fourth Presbyterian Church to catch up with the fact that physically challenged or handicapped persons have a very difficult time of it and that physical and architectural barriers become a potent psychological force that denies their humanity and assaults their identity as persons. Ralph Adam Cram and Howard Van Doren Shaw, the architects of Fourth Presbyterian Church, designed elegant buildings, but it never occurred to them that someone might want to attend worship or a meeting in the church building in a wheelchair or on crutches, for that matter. In the three buildings that comprise Fourth Church's facility, there were five separate levels that could be negotiated only by steps. For the 1,500-seat sanctuary there was one toilet, in a tiny closet, in front of the chancel, not handicapped accessible.

The few brave souls who persisted in attending Fourth Church in their wheelchairs did so with graciousness and determination, but with just enough occasionally abrasive anger to remind the staff and members that our building was terribly exclusive physically. My own personal experience on crutches following hip surgery taught me a lesson each one of us should somehow learn, namely, how painfully difficult our older buildings can be for the physically challenged and how much easier it is to stay at home than to subject oneself to the demeaning humiliation that results from trying to overcome the multiple and sometimes embarrassing hurdles in one's path.

Happily, our facility will be accessible to all when our current restoration and recreation of facilities project is completed. It will be possible for our wheelchair members to attend every event, comfortably and safely, by way of elevators and ramps. More important, as we began to talk about the issue and held meetings with the people most directly affected—the physically challenged themselves—they and we began to feel better about the inclusiveness of our community. Many of them began to attend worship regularly simply because the church had started, modestly enough, to discuss the problem. For them, it was a receptive gesture, and something of their dignity, identity, and original glory was restored.

The most insidious force that denies the humanity of men and women continues to be racism. Cornel West, an African-American scholar and author, in his important book, *Race Matters*, says that the fundamental crisis in black America is twofold: too much poverty and too little self-esteem.

West critiques his own community for buying into the self-degrading images of black people and the nihilism, hopelessness, and lovelessness that result—the "pervasive spiritual impoverishment, the collapse of meaning in life, the eclipse of hope and the absence of love of self and others . . . which leads to the cultural denudement of urban dwellers, especially children."[4]

West's comments called to mind Fourth Presbyterian Church's Center for Whole Life at Cabrini-Green: the dark halls, the glass-strewn playground, the wire caging that extends from ground level to the top of the highrises because the hallways at Cabrini are constructed on the exterior of the buildings and children kept falling to the ground. I was reminded of Dantrell Davis and the sad fact that our society will invest exactly twice as much in the education of a little boy who lives in suburban Lake Forest or Deerfield than it will in the education of a child who lives in Cabrini-Green. I was reminded of how easily we cut the budget for art, music, sports, guidance counseling at city schools—all the educational components that might add a little dignity and grace to the unbearably harsh life of a city youngster.

I was reminded of one of my son's experiences as a junior high teacher in the South Bronx. He had excelled at football, basketball, and track in high school and college, and so he agreed, as a volunteer, to organize and coach a track team at his junior high school in the Bronx. There was no track, of course. His first job was to sweep the broken whiskey bottles off the street in front of the school so that youngsters could run their wind sprints; his second, to persuade the drunks to stay away during practice. There was no equipment, no uniforms, no shoes, no showers. When he told me about his experience, I thought about the state-of-the-art athletic facilities, the artificial turf, and running surfaces now commonplace at suburban schools. And I wondered how a boy or girl at Cabrini-Green or the South Bronx can avoid learning deeply, painfully, permanently, that in relative terms, his or her life isn't worth very much.

Our church has words for this evil assault on the dignity of some: "We have offended against thy holy laws. We have left undone the things we ought to have done. O Lord, have mercy."[5]

The Word of Grace

The city is full of reminders that human dignity is assaulted on all sides: by the ideology of success that we assume for ourselves and by huge cultural forces, like ageism and racism. The church has, I believe, a redemptive word, a saving word. It needs to be said, shouted, celebrated, and lived. It is the word of grace—the incredibly good and powerful news that we are, all of us, children of God, and that in Jesus Christ, God has shown that there is nothing in creation that can interfere with God's love for each of us.

Jesus told a story about a young man and his family. This young man, not unlike countless other young men and young women, firmly believes that in order to be himself—to claim his own unique identity as a person, to say unequivocally who he is—he must make a break, must in essence reject the identity given to him by his family and community. And so he does something appalling. He goes to his father and says, in effect: "I'll never be my own man until you are dead. And since you seem pretty healthy and may be around for a while, I'd like the share of the estate that will come to me when you die. I'd like it now. I can't wait for you to die to be me."

This parent loves this child so much that he complies. The young man goes to a distant country, which the teller of the story does not identify because "distant country" simply means a place that is not in any way one's family, community, or identity; there he commences to be himself, with a vengeance. Things go badly. He loses all his money, becomes essentially a homeless bum. And then he comes to himself; he remembers who he is. And so he goes home to his parents, who have never stopped loving him. They are waiting, and his father sees him coming and runs down the road and opens his arms and embraces his child.

That story has been painted, sculpted, choreographed, and set to music thousands of times—particularly that moment of reunion. Theologian Henri Nouwen has written a book in which he reflects on Rembrandt's famous painting, *The Return of the Prodigal Son*, which hangs in the Hermitage.

Nouwen helped me to understand that the young man's leaving home is much more than a random incident. It symbolizes the personal reality that each of us, in some way, tries to leave home—not simply our parental home but our spiritual home as well. Each of us tries to forget that we belong to God, that there is one who loves us and wants us and is waiting for us to remember and to come home.

In Rembrandt's painting, the son is thin, worn, tired; his head is shaven like a prisoner's or a refugee's. The distant far country is where we go to try to forget who we are, where we listen to voices that sound attractive and seductive, but that drive out the sound of the voice that says, "I love you—you are my beloved daughter, my beloved son."

And Nouwen helped me see a wonderful detail in that great painting. The pathetic son, clothed in rags, kneeling in the embrace of his own father, curiously still has fastened to his waistband an elegant, rather valuable, short sword. This incongruity—he obviously has nothing else to call his own—says Nouwen, is the symbol of his nobility. "Whatever he had lost, money, friends, reputation, self-respect, inner peace and joy, he had not lost his parents' love. Though he was nothing else—he was his father's son."[6]

It is the deepest yearning of the human spirit, no matter where we have gone, how much or how little we have achieved, how vigorously we have asserted ourselves. There is within each of us a yearning to be what we were created to be: God's child, God's son, God's daughter—crowned with glory.

The story Jesus told was about a steadfast, unconditional love, accessible to every man and woman—to the pharisees and scribes and also to tax collectors and prostitutes about whom they complained; to CEOs and sanitation workers, young and old—the steady, accepting love of the one who created us.

That is the first word the church has for the city: grace. The second word, which I describe in chapter 7, is responsibility. The trajectory of faith is from God's unconditional gift to our living response, from grace to responsibility.

7

The Trajectory of Faith: From Grace to Responsibility

It pleased God the Father, Son, and Holy Ghost, for the manifestation of the glory of his eternal power, wisdom, and goodness, in the beginning, to create or make of nothing the world, and all things therein, whether visible or invisible, in the space of six days, and all very good.

After God had made all other creatures, he created man, male and female, with reasonable and immortal souls, endued with knowledge, righteousness, and true holiness after his own image, having the law of God written in their hearts, and power to fulfill it . . . .
—Westminster Confession of Faith, *Book of Confessions*
6.022, 6.023, PC (USA)

Each Christian is called to be a servant of God in all of life, so that we must seek God's will for the work we do and for the manner in which we do it. Christian vocation may be found in any words when our abilities and interest best meet the legitimate needs of God's world. The range of Christian responsibility is as wide as human life.
—*A Brief Statement of Belief*,
Presbyterian Church in the United States, 1962

Mankind's sole salvation lies in everyone making everything his business.[1]
—Aleksandr Solzhenitsyn

The seekers who are coming to our churches are looking for two things: affirmation and purpose. The Reformed tradition has a particular word for both these quests. The tradition is a lively and relevant foundation and an unexpected source of the imagination and energy required for church renewal. Seekers who come to church should hear two words every Sunday:

The word of responsibility. There is work for you to do. Precisely because you are a beloved child of God there is work for you to do. Your status as God's beloved implies God's confidence in you, God's reliance on you. God has given you responsibilities for your own life and, with your neighbor, responsibility for the life of your community and, with your fellow citizens, responsibility for the life of the nation and, with your fellow human beings, responsibility for the life of the world. You have important work to do, a vocation.

The word of grace. You are loved. You are a child of God. God loves you as a mother loves her nursing infant and as a father loves the returning prodigal. God loves you more than you are able to imagine. In Jesus Christ nothing can separate you from that love; nothing about you, nothing you do or fail to do, not even your own death can separate you from God's love.

The Word of Responsibility

To be a Christian in the Reformed tradition is to have a particular attitude about the world and about the God-given role human beings are to play in the world; this means Christians need both a theology and an anthropology.

Under the strong influence of Greek culture and philosophy, Christianity has always experienced a dualism, what theologian Douglas John Hall calls an "abiding ambiguity about this world." To some, dualism is a root of the problem in the church today. Classic Greek dualism maintained that reality was divided into two distinct spheres: (1) the material sphere, represented by life, which is mortal and always in the process of decaying; by the human body and its mysterious functions; and by time, which is running out; and (2) the spiritual sphere, represented by eternity, which is the absence of time; by the spirit, which is the absence of the body and its mysterious functions; by heaven, which is an ethereal place not in this world; and by a time that begins after life in this world is over.

The biblical doctrine of creation's fall and Adam and Eve's sin seemed to parallel, or at least complement, the dualism of Greek philosophy with the result that Christian history is the story of the church's trying to decide whether the world is to be loved or hated, whether the trajectory of the Christian life is into the world or withdrawal from that world, whether the Christian life—vocation—was this-worldly and secular or otherworldly and holy.

Part of what the Protestant Reformation recovered for the church was the biblical doctrine of creation and human responsibility for creation. And the most relevant dimension of the Reformed tradition today is the way the tradition defines the world and the culture in which we live and the human role in them.

The Bible is not ambiguous about the world: "And God said, 'Let the waters under the sky be gathered together into one place, and let the dry land appear.' And it was so. God called the dry land Earth, and the waters that were gathered together he called Seas. And God saw that it was good" (Gen. 1:9–10). This phrase, "and God saw that it was good," occurs seven times on the first page of the Bible. The seventh time, at the end of the process of creation, after human beings have been fashioned, male and female, in God's image, blessed, given dominion, the writer punctuates the goodness with a superlative: "God saw everything that he had made, and indeed, it was very good" (Gen. 1:31). It's almost as if the biblical writer knows that people are going to have trouble with this idea, are going to have difficulty believing that the world and all of creation is good, are going to be tempted to adopt the opposite conclusion, the Greek dualistic notion that the created order is at best suspect, at worst evil and sinful. It's almost as if the writer knows Christians are going to characterize faithful living as "otherworldly" and "unfaithful" living as "worldly."

What the Reformation recovered was the sense that human beings have a God-given assignment, or calling, to live faithfully in the world, which is, after all, a very good place to live.

That theme is there from the beginning, in the second chapter of the creation story in Genesis. It's actually a different creation story with a different point than the story in Genesis 1. In Genesis 1 the point is the goodness of creation. The point of this second creation story is human responsibility or, as it soon turns out, human irresponsibility.

In this second account, human beings are created first, and from the beginning there is a big difference between them and the rest of the created order. God fashions them, blows breath into them, and then, alone of all the creatures, speaks to them. These beings are created for conversation, dialogue, relationship.

God, both stories declare, creates human beings in the image of God, creates them with the goodness of creation in them. It is our original glory. And God gives these creatures a job to do: to live faithfully in the creation, to exercise dominion. This is our original responsibility. Before we find mention of sin or wrongdoing or guilt or culpability in the Bible, we read about grace and responsibility.

When things go wrong, as they soon do in the story, it is very much a matter of responsibility—or the human refusal to exercise the responsibility God has given and expects.

Given the garden to enjoy, Adam and Eve (whose names mean "all of us") quickly disregard the basic rules of the place and abdicate their responsibility. Eve lets a snake talk her into eating forbidden fruit. Adam lets Eve talk him into it. When they are confronted by God, Adam blames Eve: "The woman whom you gave to be with me, she gave me fruit from the tree, and I ate" (Gen. 3:12). Eve blames the snake: "The serpent tricked me, and I ate" (Gen. 3:13). That is to say, not only are human beings willful and proud, they are also unwilling to live up to their glory and their responsibility.

The creation accounts and the original sin of Adam and Eve have always had about them the hint of inappropriate sexuality. There is, after all, that business about walking around naked in the Garden. Somehow what has been conveyed to many of us was that whatever Adam and Eve did wrong must have been sexual. And so it is an important and relevant step when we read the Bible openly, without preconceived notions about the world and humankind's role in it, and discover that the world is good, human beings have a job to do, and original sin looks and sounds a lot like irresponsibility, a refusal to live up to God's expectations.

The ancient church had a perfectly good word for it—"sloth." The old Prayer of Confession says this: "We confess our sinful nature, prone to evil and slothful in good." I think that is a very helpful sentence. The human predicament is not simply that we are vain, selfish, and egocentric too full of ourselves for our own good but something of the opposite as well. We don't think highly enough of ourselves, don't look high enough, don't know ourselves as responsible moral agents placed here in God's good world, with God's image on us, God's confidence in us, and the work of God's creation before us.

Sloth, which comes from a Greek word that means "not caring," was one of the seven deadly sins. Sloth is more than simple laziness. It is the failure to love deeply, care passionately, and live responsibly. This failure goes deeper than merely electing to be a "couch potato." It is, rather, the intentional decision to be uninvolved in the world around you, and that has enormous implications. Whenever totalitarianism raises its head, as it did in Germany in the 1930s, as it did in the totalitarian Marxist regimes of eastern Europe after World War II, and as it does today with the surprising strength of the neo-Nazis and skinheads, it is because women and men elect to be uninvolved, to not care, to not be responsible for the life of the world.

One chacteristic of life in our culture at this time—particularly life in the cities but increasingly in suburbia and rural America as well—is a demcaned, devalued quality of life. The 1995 motion picture *Pulp Fiction*, which many critics thought was the most important film of the year, was incredibly, unrelentingly, and gratuitously violent. It is, at the same time, a funny movie. Its value and importance, I believe, is that it held up a mirror to our culture, and when we looked in the mirror we saw ourselves laughing at violence, trivializing human life. *Pulp Fiction* taught us the ease with which otherwise decent, caring people can be lulled into not caring about human life.

Television programming continues to produce a relentless barrage of violence: killing, pillaging, burning, raping— an evening's entertainment. In the meantime, life in the world, particularly in the city, seems to have diminishing value.

Cornel West argues in *Race Matters* that the incredible violence that characterizes life in urban ghettos arises from a sense that life has no value. In turn, that same valuelessness contributes to more violence. West thinks a nihilism pervades urban African-American communities, which he describes as the experience of "coping with a life of horrifying meaninglessness, hopelessness, and lovelessness. The frightening result is a numbing detachment from others and a self-destructive disposition toward the world."[2] Theologian Douglas John Hall agrees that our culture is producing a "covert nihilism" which results when people give up the possibility of hope.[3]

Even as I write these words, the Illinois juvenile justice system is agonizing over what to do with the eleven- and twelve-year-old boys who dropped a four-year-old to his death from the window of an empty apartment in the Ida B. Wells housing complex. The youthful offenders, confined to a juvenile custody facility, remain intransigent, and quarrelsome and continue to exhibit violent tendencies.

From purposelessness to valuelessness to nihilism to violence has become a distressing reality in the city.

The late Karl Menninger twenty years ago wrote the influential book *Whatever Became of Sin?*, in which he argued that there is something about life in the last half of the twentieth century that has reduced the significance, autonomy, and responsibility of the individual. Life seems to be in the hands of large cosmic forces inaccessible to the lone individual. Instead of feeling like empowered actors on the stage of history, we feel like victims. The result, he maintained, is the end of personal responsibility. Whatever goes wrong is someone else's fault; it was caused by the infamous "them."

Too many guns? Children killing children in our streets? Not my problem.

Public schools underfunded, understaffed, over-bureaucratized? Not my fault.

My nation's mortality rate at nineteenth in the world for children under five? Not my fault.

The people who come to the churches are searching for grace and, I believe, for responsibility. The Reformed tradition focuses on both.

Vocation: Tradition and Transformation

Our doctrine of vocation is, I believe, the point at which the tradition encounters the world with transforming power and life-changing relevance. Until the Reformation, the word *vocation*, which comes from a Latin word meaning "calling," referred to clergy. To have a vocation was to join a monastery or convent, to separate oneself intentionally and dramatically from the everyday life of the world. I've always thought that the most revolutionary idea in the world was the Reformed notion of vocation: that every man and woman has a calling, a job to do; that each of us is called by God to love the world, to care passionately about our own lives and the life of our community; and that God gives to each of us responsibility for our own lives and the life of the world.

It's not merely a Chamber of Commerce kind of cheerleading for us. It's a matter of our basic theological framework. We believe the world is a good place because God created it that way. We believe God calls us to life in the world and that it is there—in our everyday lives, at work, in our families and intimate relationships, in our leisure-time pursuits—we are called to serve God and to be responsible for creation.

Billy Graham has said that there are two commissions: the first calls us to come to Jesus Christ; the second sends us, in Christ's name, into the world.

The Reformed tradition suggests that it is one commission: to

Jesus Christ and to the world God creates and loves—and for which Christ died.

Sometimes the commission to the world, the decision to be a responsible participant in the life of the world, actually precedes a personal commitment to Jesus Christ. In fact, I see it frequently in earnest young adults who volunteer in one of the outreach ministries at Fourth Presbyterian Church: cooking for the homeless, rehabilitating apartments at Cabrini-Green, building a house with Habitat for Humanity, tutoring a child. Typically, the volunteer has not been to a traditional church worship service for years, hasn't been in a church except for friends' weddings, hasn't taken the traditional church seriously for a long time, but has decided that her or his life lacks something. They have acknowledged that the busy, hectic, insular world of business leaves one exhausted and empty, and so they decide to volunteer to do some good for other people. And in the process of helping and serving other human beings, they begin to care—to love, even—and that process of becoming responsible becomes a channel, an opening to the heart. A connection is made between this human being I am helping, the church that has made the connection, and the Lord of the church, whose love for the world inspired it and guides and directs it.

People are looking for affirmation and for a purpose for their lives. The search for a vocation is, I believe, an important part of what contemporary seekers are seeking. There was a time when faithful women and men would have chosen to be faithful to God by withdrawing from the everyday life of the world. But when we embrace this Reformed tradition of ours and let it speak to us and live through us, our faithfulness to God leads more deeply and passionately into the life of the world:

> Susan heard God's call to be responsible, took a leave of absence from her job in a state agency as an occupational therapist, and spent a year in Romania, working in an orphanage.
>
> Emily, an R.N., heard God's call to be responsible and signed up for a tour of duty in a Christian hospital in Rwanda.
>
> Jack and Joy heard God's call to be responsible for life in the world and used their vacations from newspaper work and a healthcare agency to travel to Nicaragua and work in projects sponsored by a Nicaraguan Council of Churches.
>
> Scott heard the call to be responsible and volunteered to be a tutor.

Larry, the dean of the graduate school of education in one of our local universities, heard the call to put professional aspirations responsibly on hold, and agreed to be a private consultant to the all-important process of public school reform.

Ann moved her law practice from a prestigious local law firm to the Pentagon because she heard God's call to responsibility.

As Czechoslovakia was throwing off the yoke of totalitarianism, Vaclav Havel, who would soon become the President of the new Czech Republic, was invited to address the United States Congress. His words have been quoted many times. They should be required reading for us all as we move into an uncertain future. They are words all Christians should understand:

> The salvation of this human world lies nowhere else than in the human heart . . . in human responsibility . . . . Responsibility for something higher than my family, my firm, my country, my success—responsibility to the order of being when all our actions are indelibly recorded and where and only where they will be properly judged.

For people searching for meaning, people not sure their lives have much purpose, people struggling with a sense of personal insignificance, the Reformed tradition has two powerful and saving words:

> The world is a good place because God created it and loves it.

> You have important work to do because you are God's child, God's beloved.

What calls responsibility out of us, as individuals and as churches, is a new sense of God's love, God's amazing grace that seeks us out and claims us and reminds us of who we are and whose we are. It is a love that picks us up, dusts us off, reminds us that we are God's beloved children, and then sends us into the world to new tasks or to our old tasks as responsible moral agents, God's people.

From grace to responsibility.

8

The Church in the Future: Coherence, Experience, Relevance

And I tell you, you are Peter, and on this rock I will build my church, and the gates of Hades will not prevail against it.
—Matthew 16:18

I believe in the . . . holy catholic Church . . . .
—The Apostles' Creed, *Book of Confessions* 2.3, PC(USA)

Congregations are durable and have become ever more interesting to social historians because they have an integrity of their own, however ambivalent their postures and ambiguous their intentions and achievements may be.[1]
— Martin E. Marty

The congregation as a church or embodiment of a church is of necessity a religious entity as well as a sociological one, a locus of the sacred or the holy as well as an embodiment, however unique, of human relationship. If, therefore, we are to understand the congregation as a representation of the church, we must also reflect on how it is a religious entity, or, in special Christian language, how it is that God or God's grace acts in, is present to, or empowers this community.[2]
—Langdon Gilkey

The time of the congregation has come. The historians and sociologists of religion who are studying the church and writing books are concluding that the local church, the congregation, is where the energy is located. And it is where the hope for the future will be found.

There was a time when we defined church as a national organization with a national identity, a national staff, a national mission program, and a national headquarters. For some of us the opportunity to visit the national offices of our church, occupying several

floors of a multiple-story office building in Manhattan, at 475
Riverside Drive, was a spiritual pilgrimage. And the names of the
people who worked in those offices, the executive secretaries and
directors of global and national programs, filled us with admiration,
respect, and confidence. There was also a time when the people who
study and analyze the church were saying that the future of the
church's mission would be found in ecumenical and community-
based para-church organizations, industrial institutes, in ecumenical
consortia. Local and state councils of churches played a prominent
role in their respective communities, attracting creative leadership
and strong financial support.

Today, church headquarters are no longer in New York City.
The continuing reduction in financial support for denominational
mission programs has necessitated major downsizing in national
staff and curtailment of nationally funded mission activity. Most of
the para-church organizations are gone, and the ecumenical organizations are fighting for their lives.

What remains of the old church establishment is the congregation, the local church. I'm not ready to give up on denominations
and denominational programs—far from it. Plenty of creativity
remain in the national structures, although the people who work in
them are inclined to be victims of the renewed ideological struggle
within the church, and they must spend much, if not most, of their
time and energy answering charges from their opponents, justifying
their existence, and worrying about whether they will have a job
next year. Instead of criticizing bureaucracy and blaming them for
everything that is wrong with the church, I think we ought to give
every employee of the national church structures an award for
courage, patience, and service beyond the call of duty. They are a
source of hope for the future and a resource that the church must
preserve and protect.

There is plenty of life left in the denominations as national structures. The same is true for the remaining ecumenical organizations.

The National Council of Churches of Christ, the target of unre-
lenting attacks by ideological critics from the far right, continues to
represent its member communions in ministries of education, disas-
ter relief, justice and public advocacy. National Council of Churches
Executive Secretary Joan Brown Campbell is an articulate, courageous, and strong spokesperson in the public arena for the cause of
Christ, and she is a respected and credible representative of all the
churches.

I believe, however, that a shift in energy has occurred from the national to the local, from national structures to local congregations. Mission is happening locally. Congregations are looking at their own communities with renewed mission focus and planning and implementing new mission initiatives. National structures are working not so much to mount programs on behalf of the congregations but to support, resource, and empower local congregations to do their own mission. There will always be mission programs that must be coordinated and funded by a national organization. Creative and strong leadership will always be required to produce educational materials for the congregations. But the ground has shifted. The energy is coming from the congregations.

The congregation is where I have invested my life for thirty-three years. Theologian Langdon Gilkey says that we must begin to see the congregation not merely as a sociological phenomenon but as a "religious entity," which he defines as a "locus of the sacred . . . an embodiment of human relationships . . . a place where God's grace acts and God is present."[3]

I love the congregation because it is all that and much, much more. Whenever I am away from the church for several weeks I miss it, feeling first an uneasy emptiness and then a full-throttle longing on Sunday morning. When I am on the job, I love walking to work in the morning, past the gothic building on Michigan Avenue, a silent testimony to the holy in the city. I love walking home at night knowing that the church's ministries of outreach, education, counseling, tutoring, prayer meetings, Bible study, and Twelve-Step recovery programs will continue until the lights are turned off and the doors locked at 10:00 P.M. I look forward to the church's public worship with mounting eagerness all week long until Sunday morning, the Lord's Day, when the church will gather to sing and pray and be together.

The church is, I conclude, God's great gift to us. And though many of us have a lifelong lover's quarrel with it—wanting it to be all that it can be, impatient and irritated when it is not—nonetheless the church is Christ's body in the world, the institutional expression of the incarnation, the specific place where, on regular occasions the Word becomes flesh.

Last Sunday morning it happened all over again at the Fourth Presbyterian Church of Chicago and also in thousands of other congregations in cities and towns and villages across the country. It was Baptism Sunday. We baptize infants on the second Sunday of every month, and because of the configuration of our chancel area, but also to preserve as much of the individuality of the occasion as possible, we limit the number of baptisms at each worship service to six. Lately, we've been having more requests for infant baptism than the policy accommodates. It is the happy result of our membership growth, primarily in young adults who marry and begin their families in the city. It is also because more and more couples are remaining in the city to raise their children, a result the original designers of urban church buildings like ours did not anticipate. We have just completed the construction of a large, modern, well-lighted and well-supplied accessible nursery, complete with electronic beepers for each parent to carry into the sanctuary in case a child needs parental attention. Fortunately, the beepers do not actually beep but signal by way of a gentle vibration.

Last Sunday there were two baptisms at 8:30 A.M. and seven more at 11:00 A.M. The parents sat in front on a row of special chairs, with proud grandparents, aunts, uncles, and friends in the pews directly behind. Seven infants will attract quite a crowd of beaming, happy, and proud relatives. The ministers, facing the congregation, can see this wonderfully human tableaux, can observe the faces of the parents, for whom it is an occasion of extraordinary meaning. It is, I always find myself thinking, an extraordinarily important and hopeful occasion for the church as well.

Last Sunday as I surveyed the line of proud parents and babies across the front of the sanctuary, I noticed that one woman holding her baby was by herself. This is not altogether unusual, and it occurs for a variety of reasons. But as I looked at her and noted the emotion on her face, I remembered her story. She is single, a professional woman. Her baby daughter is Chinese. She had traveled to China alone, and after weeks of very difficult negotiating, living in incredibly arduous circumstances, she had returned with a baby girl. I know that many people, particularly the governments of the nations themselves, are wondering about the advisability of this whole cross-cultural adoption process. But there she was in the front of the sanctuary, fifteen hundred people there for the occasion, to witness her daughter's initiation into the community of Christ. And as I cradled tiny Sarah Rose in my arms and sprinkled the waters of baptism on her head and said, "Sarah, child of God, you are sealed by the Holy Spirit in baptism, and you belong to Jesus Christ forever," I was struck by the wonder of it all—this congregation in the middle of a busy American city, and this tiny Chinese baby, held now in the arms of a congregation, a family of faith, that promised to be the church for her, to represent and provide God's love and grace for her. Forty minutes later, when we stood to sing the closing hymn, *Lift High the Cross,* Sarah Rose was still there, sound asleep now, having enjoyed a bottle and a long nap during my sermon and the rest of the service. My wonder returned as we sang these words:

> Each newborn servant of the Crucified
> Bears on the brow the seal of Christ who died.
> Lift high the cross, the love of Christ proclaim
> Till all the world adore His sacred name.

After worship, and over coffee, I greeted Scott and Lisa, and inquired about their lively oldest daughter, Melissa, aged twelve. We've been worrying about and praying for Melissa, Scott, and Lisa for several months, ever since Melissa was diagnosed with a rare neurological condition that was causing sudden, dangerous, and difficult seizures. After weeks and weeks of arduous examinations and testing at a number of hospitals that specialize in children's neurological disorders, a diagnosis was made and surgery prescribed— highly sophisticated, delicate, and very risky brain surgery. We surrounded them as best we could with pastoral care, visited and telephoned regularly, elected one of us to travel to St. Louis, where the surgery was performed, to be with them during the critical period, and, of course, prayed for them every day when the staff gathered to begin the workday with morning prayers. The surgery had gone beautifully. A piece of Melissa's skull was removed, and the surgeon probed deeply inside the tissue of the brain and removed a lesion that was causing the seizures. A day later Melissa was sitting up in bed, chatting brightly. Now they were back in church—grateful, almost unspeakably grateful for the surgeon's skill, for the church's love, for God's grace and love.

"How's she doing at school" I asked.

"She's an athlete, you know," Lisa told me, "but until her head is completely mended she can't play contact sports, so she's on the track team now, running the mile, wearing her helmet!"

Jack and Wes are waiting to see me. Jack has HIV/AIDS, and so far, with the help of massive doses of very expensive drugs, is managing to carry on. He and Wes are in worship every Sunday. I first heard about Jack when he told one of our ministers that he needed to make eight trips to a hospital a thousand miles from Chicago for a new drug therapy that had been prescribed. He had no way to pay for the air fare. We put the word out and by the end of the week we had received more than enough frequent flyer miles for four roundtrip tickets. Jack and Wes are interested to know what the church is saying about them. They are, for the first time in their lives, I think, experiencing the church as something less than condemning, and sometimes even accepting and affirming. They want me to know that they are there in the coffee hour and that they are grateful for the church.

As I make my way to my office, a young woman finds me and wants me to know about what happened to her grandmother. She is an internist at Cook County Hospital. Her grandmother, Mrs. Carlisle, is in her nineties. It seems that a few weeks earlier, on the coldest day of the winter, when the temperature stood at 15 degrees below zero, Mrs. Carlisle decided to keep her weekly hair appointment at her favorite beauty parlor in the loop, two miles away from her apartment. For some reason she got off the bus at the wrong stop and, oblivious to the dangerously low temperature, started to walk in the direction of the beauty parlor. After a short distance, she began to experience difficulty and became confused. The raw wind, howling between tall buildings, added danger to the already extremely low temperature, and she began to suffer hypothermia. Mrs. Carlisle had the good sense to stop at a small shop when she realized she was becoming disoriented. She could not remember her address or even where she was headed. When the concerned clerk asked whether she had anything in her handbag that might help identify her, Mrs. Carlisle pulled out a small business card from Fourth Presbyterian Church with our telephone number on it. The clerk called the church. The receptionist forwarded the call to our social service center. The director himself hopped into a cab, drove to the loop, gathered up Mrs. Carlisle, and accompanied her to her apartment. Her young physician granddaughter assured me that Mrs. Carlisle had fully recovered, with no after-effects, from her harrowing adventure and that the entire family was grateful for the presence of the church in the city and in their lives.

In his book *Claiming the Center*,[4] theologian and church leader Jack Rogers says that the image of the church as an "ark of salvation" retains its relevance and vitality.

Langdon Gilkey agrees. In strongly descriptive words that could be written for many churches I know, he observes this:

The "secular" picture of a secular order now free from the former ravages of religion is a dream. Present secular society is redolent of anxieties of all sorts: its personal sins of abuse, of radical self-interest, of materialism, and of greed not only destroy individuals and families alike but overflow into our national environment. . . . People are hassled, anxious, guilty, lonely, tortured by their personal vices, their isolation from others, their impending deaths, and by the stark meaninglessness of their existence.[5]

Gilkey says that for all this, what is needed is "a supportive community, a community to rescue them from themselves, their talents, their weaknesses, their life—the church not as contracted communities, but as Ark, the church where finitude, fate, sin, and death are articulated, confessed and resolved through grace."[6]

The church of the future will be, I believe, vital congregations whose witness will be coherent, whose life will be experiential, and whose programs and mission will be intentionally relevant.

Coherence

O God, you are my God, I seek you,
    my soul thirsts for you;
my flesh faints for you,
    as in a dry and weary land where there is no water.
                                    (Psalm 63:1)

We are a generation of seekers: the quest for meaning, for intimacy, for transcendence, for God is perhaps the dominant dimension of contemporary American life. The culture keeps asking the basic questions of faith. In early 1996, a popular song with the intriguing title "What If God Was One of Us" earned Grammy nominations, and a motion picture about a nun who makes a strong Christian witness in the midst of a condemned murderer's final journey to his execution has earned the actress, Susan Sarandon, an Academy Award. And John Updike has just produced another bestseller that some reviewers think is his finest work, *In the Beauty of the Lilies*, a novel about faith, meaning, and belief in postmodern, post-Christian America.

Part of the thirst for God evidenced in American culture and described two and a half millennia ago in Psalm 63 ("I seek you, my soul thirsts for you") is, I know, intellectual. Modern Americans long for a religion that is coherent, a religion that does not provide slick, easy answers to the perplexing dilemmas of modern life but does at least know what the questions are, and is not hesitant to engage the questions, to bring the questions into the church, to enable the dramatic interchange between gospel and culture.

When the Presbyterian Church (U.S.A.) General Assembly gathered in Wichita in the hot summer of 1994, Presbyterians were afraid that the church might split apart. At issue was the denomination's involvement in an ecumenical conference, Re-Imagining God—Community—Church, held as part of the World Council of Church's Ecumenical Decade of Solidarity with Women. Some thought the conference violated the boundaries of Christian theology. Others thought the conference was a creative, supportive, and faithful celebration of the gospel's radical transforming and liberating power. I was privileged to be an elected commissioner to that assembly and was appointed by the Moderator of the General Assembly to serve as moderator of the committee that was assigned the task of dealing with the controversy—of sorting out the issues and coming up with a healing proposal. What was both fascinating and telling about the experience of the Presbyterian Church (U.S.A.) at Wichita in the summer of 1994 was the way the church came together around a simple phrase, "theology matters."

That was the theme of the committee's report, which the General Assembly approved by a 97-percent margin—an unheard-of consensus among Presbyterians! The report affirmed that what we believe matters, that the content of Christian faith is important, that we are grateful for and expect coherence in our religion. Neither the committee nor the assembly said that there is only one theology that matters, but rather that the process of doing theology through study and teaching of our own Reformed tradition, the ecumenical conversation between our theological traditions and others, and the handing down of our theological tradition to our children and grandchildren are very high priorities for Presbyterians.

The report was the product of a diverse and faithful group of fifty-five Presbyterians from all over the country, who at the end of an arduous and demanding five days of work sent the report to the assembly with its unanimous support. Each of those participants has a favorite paragraph, section, or sentence in the report, I imagine. My favorite is the reference to handing a church and a theological tradition down to our children and grandchildren. I have children, five of them, and grandchildren, four at present, and they have in one way or another been recipients of and been formed and nurtured by the church and its theological tradition.

The church of the future will be congregationally based, and it will know that its theology matters, that its people want a coherent faith, which is another way of saying that they thirst for God.

Experience

So I have looked upon you in the sanctuary,
   beholding your power and glory.
                    (Psalm 63:2)

A congregation, according to Langdon Gilkey, is a "religious entity, a locus of the sacred." And so the vital congregation—urban or rural, small or large—will recall that the precious gift the church has to give the world is the presence of God. It's not that the church owns or controls God or God's presence. It is that modernity sometimes forgets the presence, takes its "secularity" altogether too seriously.

Don Benedict, the legendary leader of the Chicago City Missionary Society during the turbulent sixties and seventies, is credited with saying that "the basic task of the city church is to keep alive the rumor that there is a God." I've been quoting that wonderful line for years. After coming to Chicago, I had the great privilege of meeting Don Benedict for lunch, and I asked him whether he had actually said that "the basic task of the city church is to keep alive the rumor that there is a God." Benedict admitted he wasn't sure, that many people attributed it to him and that if he hadn't said it he wished he had, because it is true!

It is, of course, the task not only of city churches but of all the churches today, to keep alive the rumor, to bear witness to the presence, to proclaim in word, mission, and the quality of the institutional life it lives that all human life is blessed by, accountable to, and lived out in the presence of God.

There are many ways to do it but chief among them, I believe, is our tradition of worship. Our liturgies, our music, our praying, and our preaching must be planned thoughtfully and presented carefully. The ministry of worship is where most people experience the presence of the holy, the sacred in the midst of life, or at least they are quiet and reflective long enough to be open to experience it.

It is a precious gift. Not only the future of the churches but the life of our communities and the larger culture itself need and depend on it.

Relevance

Because your steadfast love is better than life,
my lips will praise you.
(Psalm 63:3)

The day of the church as sacred enclave, cloistered, withdrawn from the world intellectually, aesthetically, politically, and socially, is over. The church of the future will be connected openly, intentionally, and unapologetically to the world around it.

We keep discovering at Fourth Presbyterian Church and want to share with everybody the idea that mission is evangelism, that modern Americans find the work the church is willing to venture in the world a compelling reason to join the church. Jesus said, "Come to me." He also said, "Go into all the world." The two are not mutually exclusive. The two mandates may address us or our congregations at different times in our histories, but Jesus said them both, and in some way, I believe the churches must hear and heed them both.

The people who attend the new-member classes at Fourth Presbyterian Church tell us that they are joining the church and hearing the gospel, perhaps for the first time, because the life of the church means something to its own members and also to the life of the city. "Belonging here adds up to something," one young securities trader said recently.

Vital churches in the future will care about their communities at least as much as they care about themselves and their own survival. It is not always an easy lesson to learn, particularly when the survival of the enterprise seems to be at risk and in doubt. But this caring remains the vital, life-giving component. Every congregation, no matter how large or small, no matter how modest or magnificent its facility, can and must identify its mission—the work in the world to which Jesus Christ calls it—and then do it. It may mean the creation of new programs to tutor a few youngsters or to provide meals on wheels. It may mean signing up with Habitat for Humanity to help build one new low-cost home. It may mean providing free space for local Alcoholics Anonymous weekly meetings. It may mean using the church building for a desperately needed daycare center or nursery school.

No one could, or should, promise success. Christ calls the church to be faithful, not successful. But I can bear witness to my own experience that there is something about seeing the congregation in terms of its mission that is transforming to the congregation itself. There is something about mission that is energizing and life-giving. "I'm joining this church," the securities trader said, "even though I haven't darkened the door of a church for ten years because when the bell goes off at the end of the day, this place has added something of value to the life of the city."

I'm hopeful about the church of the future. In the midst of all the handwringing about the decline of mainline religion, I find liveliness and reasons for confidence. The Reformed tradition itself is the source of a creative future for the church because of its insistence that the church's life is lived in the world and in conversation with the world. That means always that to the degree the churches are faithful to the tradition, they will be energetically and imaginatively engaged with the world.

My experience is that there is compelling power in that engagement with the world. I have come to understand that it is the same compelling power that attracted the crowds of people to the one who came preaching and teaching and healing, the one who confounded the expectations of his people by living thoroughly in the world, walking their dusty roads, visiting their villages, receiving their young and old, their sick and lame, and extending to outcasts love and accepting grace.

I have hope for the church when it is faithful to its Lord. But I also dare to be hopeful because deep within our faith tradition is the confidence that God is not done yet with the process of creating this world. We remember and celebrate this concept every Advent when we hear the haunting words of the prophet Isaiah:

> Comfort, O comfort my people,
>   says your God. . . .
> Every valley shall be lifted up,
>   and every mountain and hill be made low.
>   (Isa. 40:1, 4a)

My personal faith is stirred by the annual reminder that worrying about the future is not a new experience for God's people: twenty-five hundred years ago, the people of God were convinced that the end had come and that there was no hope for the future. When the exiles in Babylon looked ahead, they saw the end of the line, the end of their culture, their precious customs and stories, their religion, and their nationhood. Because it was so painful to look ahead, they focused on the past instead, reminiscing about how it used to be in the good old days.

Great events were on the horizon. But the captives were unable to see them and get ready to respond to them because they were looking backward, living in the past. And so the prophet wrote:

Do not remember the former things,
    or consider the things of old.
I am about to do a new thing;
    now it springs forth, do you not perceive it?
                                    (Isa. 43:18–19)

Deep within our faith tradition is trust in a God who does new things, a God whose plan for creation is not yet complete. God's kingdom of justice, equality, and compassion is coming but not yet here. God continues to bring it into the life of the world. And on occasion, God's people become the agents, the instruments of the new creation, the new thing God is doing.

That is why I have hope for the future. The basic Christian affirmation is about the present and the future, not the past. It is that, in Jesus Christ, God was doing a new thing in human history. It is that God continues the process, continues to create newness. That is what the old story is about—birth, life, death, resurrection. The resurrection of Jesus Christ is not about the resuscitation of a dead body two thousand years ago. That's history. The Christian faith, the resurrection faith of the church of Jesus Christ, is about the presence of the risen Christ in our life, creating new possibilities, making all things new, establishing justice, welcoming the children, healing the sick, and binding up wounds.

Retrospect

After a long Sunday, I return to my study to plan the memorial service for Evelyn, who died last week at the age of ninety-nine, one of our oldest members. Unlike many contemporary Chicagoans, Evelyn was a native, born in the last decade of the last century. She knew by name every Fourth Presbyterian Church pastor in this century. She could recall when the new building was dedicated in 1914. She had lived in a nursing home in the same neighborhood where she was born and where she had lived, married, and gone to church for nearly a century. With failing eyesight she read every newsletter, every letter and note that came to her room from her church. She knew what was happening in the life of her church even though she had not been able to attend for twenty years. And because of the regular visits of the pastors, the lay ministry team, and the Caring Connection and, of course, because of the Sacrament of the Lord's Supper, celebrated with her in her room, she was very much a part of the family of faith.

One time, several years ago, when she was still able to walk, Evelyn wandered out the front door of the nursing home. The professional staff was frantic. She was gone for several hours on a very hot summer afternoon. Because our ministers are regular visitors in the nursing home, a receptionist remembered Evelyn's connection to Fourth Church and called us to inquire whether we knew her whereabouts. A colleague, the one who knew her best, knew exactly what to do. David walked over to the sanctuary, always open during the day, and found her sitting alone in her pew, the pew she had occupied with her family as a little girl, the pew where she had sat beside her husband for fifty years, the pew she had sat in for eighty-five years. Confused, nearly overcome with heat, Evelyn remembered the church, found it, and was found in it.

Tomorrow we will celebrate her life and God's love for her. For all of us who are privileged to belong to this place, it will also be a celebration of the church, Evelyn's home for nearly a century, and we will, I am sure, experience again the strong hope for the future of the church because of this promise:

I am about to do a new thing;
now it springs forth, do you not perceive it?
(Isa. 43:19)

Notes

Introduction

1. Douglas John Hall, *Professing the Faith: Christian Theology in a North American Context* (Minneapolis: Fortress Press, 1993), 257.

Chapter 1

1. Harvey Cox, *Fire from Heaven* (Reading, Mass.: Addision-Wesley Publishing Co., 1995), 104.
2. Ibid., 31.
3. Langdon Gilkey, "The Christian Congregation as a Religious Community," in *American Congregations: New Perspectives in the Study of Congregations*, vol. 2., ed. James P. Wind and James W. Lewis (Chicago: The University of Chicago Press, 1994), 100.
4. Ibid., 109.
5. Hans Küng, *Credo: The Apostle's Creed Explained for Today*, trans. John Bowden (New York: Doubleday, 1993), xii.

Chapter 2

1. Douglas John Hall, *Professing the Faith: Christian Theology in a North American Context* (Minneapolis: Fortress Press, 1993), 274.

Chapter 3

1. Wade Clark Roof, *A Generation of Seekers: The Spiritual Journeys of the Baby Boom Generation* (San Francisco: Harper-SanFrancisco, 1993), 4.

2. Hans Küng, *Credo: The Apostle's Creed Explained for Today*, trans. John Bowden (New York: Doubleday, 1993), 127.
3. Roof, *A Generation of Seekers*, 246.
4. Brian A. Gerrish, "Tradition in the Modern World: The Reformed Habit of Mind," from the T. V. Moore Lectures, April 19–20, 1990, San Francisco Theological Seminary.
5. Langdon Gilkey, "The Christian Congregation as a Religious Community," in *American Congregations: New Perspectives in the Study of Congregations*, vol. 2., ed. James P. Wind and James W. Lewis (Chicago: The University of Chicago Press, 1994), 108.

Chapter 4

1. Harvey Cox, *Fire from Heaven* (Reading, Mass.: Addison-Wesley Publishing Co., 1995), 306.
2. Letty M. Russell, *Becoming Human* (Philadelphia: Westminster Press, 1982), 24.
3. Ibid., 23.
4. Jacob Needleman, *Money and the Meaning of Life* (New York: Doubleday, 1991), 2.
5. Annie Dillard, *The Writing Life* (New York: Harper & Row, 1989), 78–79.

Chapter 5

1. Kathleen Norris, *Dakota: A Spiritual Journey* (New York: Ticknor & Fields, 1993), 161.

Chapter 6

1. Leonard Sweet, "Can a Mainstream Change Its Course?" in *Liberal Protestantism: Realities and Possibilities*, ed. Robert S. Michaelson and Wade Clark Roof (New York: Pilgrim Press, 1986), 242.
2. Ernest J. Gaines, *A Lesson before Dying* (New York: Random House, 1993), 7–8.
3. Joseph Sittler, *Second Opinion*, the Park Ridge [Illinois] Center Journal (July 1993): 15.
4. Cornel West, *Race Matters* (Boston: Beacon Press, 1993), 5.
5. *Book of Common Worship* (Louisville, Ky.: Westminster/John Knox Press, 1993), 87.
6. Henri Nouwen, *The Return of the Prodigal Son* (New York: Doubleday, 1992), 35, 42, 44.

Chapter 7

1. From a 1970 Nobel Prize lecture by Aleksandr Solzhenitsyn.
2. Cornel West, *Race Matters* (Boston: Beacon Press, 1993), 14.
3. Douglas John Hall, *Professing the Faith: Christian Theology in a North American Context* (Minneapolis: Fortress Press, 1993), 294.

Chapter 8

1. Martin E. Marty, "Public and Private: Congregations as Meeting Place," in *American Congregations: New Perspectives in the Study of Congregations*, vol. 2, ed. James P. Wind and James W. Lewis (Chicago: The University of Chicago Press, 1994), 162.
2. Langdon Gilkey, "The Christian Congregation as a Religious Community," in *American Congregations*, ibid., 100.
3. Ibid., 100.
4. Jack B. Rogers, *Claiming the Center* (Louisville, Ky.: Westminster John Knox Press, 1995).
5. Gilkey, *American Congregations*, 108.
6. Gilkey, ibid., 108.